T0311553

ROUTLEDGE LIBRARY EDITIONS:
URBAN AND REGIONAL ECONOMICS

Volume 22

THE ECONOMICS OF
REAL PROPERTY

THE ECONOMICS OF REAL PROPERTY
An Analysis of Property Values and Patterns of Use

RALPH TURVEY

Routledge
Taylor & Francis Group

LONDON AND NEW YORK

First published in 1957 by Allen & Unwin

This edition first published in 2018
by Routledge
2 Park Square, Milton Park, Abingdon, Oxon OX14 4RN

and by Routledge
711 Third Avenue, New York, NY 10017

Routledge is an imprint of the Taylor & Francis Group, an informa business

British Library Cataloguing in Publication Data
A catalogue record for this book is available from the British Library

ISBN: 978-1-138-09590-8 (Set)
ISBN: 978-1-315-10306-8 (Set) (ebk)
ISBN: 978-1-138-10223-1 (Volume 22) (hbk)
ISBN: 978-1-138-10257-6 (Volume 22) (pbk)
ISBN: 978-1-315-10309-9 (Volume 22) (ebk)

Publisher's Note
The publisher has gone to great lengths to ensure the quality of this reprint but points out that some imperfections in the original copies may be apparent.

Disclaimer
The publisher has made every effort to trace copyright holders and would welcome correspondence from those they have been unable to trace.

THE ECONOMICS OF
REAL PROPERTY

AN ANALYSIS OF PROPERTY VALUES
AND PATTERNS OF USE

BY

RALPH TURVEY

Reader in Economics
in the
University of London

Ruskin House
GEORGE ALLEN & UNWIN LTD
MUSEUM STREET LONDON

FIRST PUBLISHED IN 1957

PRINTED IN GREAT BRITAIN
in 12 point Fournier type
BY T. AND A. CONSTABLE LTD
EDINBURGH

TO C. L.

PREFACE

THE subject of this book has received very little attention in recent years. In the later part of the nineteenth century the case was different; property taxation, for example, was widely discussed, and many books and official reports were published. The economists of the time, including such eminent men as Cannan and Edgeworth, took their part in the debate, while many of the other participants showed themselves to be well versed in the economic literature. At present, property taxation is no longer a burning political issue and other problems such as housing subsidies and town and country planning are in the forefront. Yet most writings on these subjects show little awareness of their economic aspects; the economic analysis implicit in the Uthwatt Report, to name but one example, is very amateurish. With few exceptions, professional economists have contributed nothing in the field. The learned journals of the past few decades contain hardly any articles on land economics, and even the textbooks on pricing and distribution rarely devote any attention to the property market.

Whatever the causes of this state of affairs, it is surely deplorable. On the one hand people concerned with real estate problems, such as valuers and town planners, lack one of the essential tools for their work. On the other hand economists have done little to help them and are failing to take up interesting and important problems.

I hope to provide a stimulus to both groups in this book. Assuming a knowledge of elementary economics in the reader, I have tried to provide an analysis of the features peculiar to the property market. There are many gaps in the analysis whose removal must wait upon extensive empirical research, so this book is an introduction to the subject.

Many people have helped me; thanks are due in particular to Lucien Foldes, Carl Kaysen, Nathaniel Lichfield, Lionel Robbins,

Philip White and Basil Yamey. I am indebted to the editors of *The London and Cambridge Economic Bulletin* and *The Times Review of Industry*, *The Economic Journal* and *The Review of Economic Studies* to include previously published material in Chapter IX.

London School of Economics
October 1956

CONTENTS

CHAPTER I

INTRODUCTION

THE subject of this book is the working of the price mechanism in the property market. In the first part the determination of property values and rents and their rôle in allocating land and buildings between different uses is analysed. In the second part this analysis is applied to examine the effects of property taxation, an aspect of landlord and tenant law and the compensation-betterment problem. Except for Chapter V, the discussion is largely confined to urban property and may thus be called a study in urban land economics.

Two limitations of the treatment deserve to be noted at the start. Firstly, in discussing questions of policy I have concentrated on 'economic efficiency' in the technical sense and have neglected questions of fairness, aspects which involve value-judgements. In other words, the emphasis is on allocational problems, not on distributional problems, though signs of my beliefs may be apparent; if so, those who disagree with them can express this by saying that bias has crept in. After all, despite their preachings, many economists follow the practice of avoiding explicit value-judgements only to inject them implicitly!

A second limitation is that what follows is largely economic theory. I have not attempted a survey of British property law, property taxation or town and country planning. The aim of the book is to provide a background, to work out an analytical approach for the study of these matters, so they are referred to only to illustrate the argument. Nor have I incorporated much in the way of empirical investigations, though it would be desirable to cite case-studies in order to test, to quantify or to exemplify the analysis. The sad fact is that information is difficult to obtain

I

and that relatively few economists have done work in this field—
at least so far as regards urban property. Thus I have had very
little material to draw upon.

Most of the research that has been done in urban land
economics in recent years has been American, and there are even
a few American textbooks on urban land economics. The most
recent of these is *Urban Real Estate* by Ernest and Robert M.
Fisher (Henry Holt, 1954), which summarizes and refers to most
of the important literature. In contrast to the present work it
contains a good deal of descriptive material, but the authors
hardly attempt much deductive analysis of the sort presented
here. The reader who wishes to survey the American contribu-
tions cannot do better than to refer to this work, from chapter 10
onwards.

Interests in Property

From the point of view of economic theory, real property is
one among several types of factor of production, so the general
theory of the pricing and allocation of the factors of production
applies to it. But this theory is too general to cover all that can
be interestingly said on the subject. Just as labour has sufficient
peculiarities to justify labour economics as a separate branch of
study, so the heterogeneity, indivisibility and institutional
peculiarities of real property make some separate treatment worth
while. The subject deserves, but often fails to get, a separate
chapter in the textbooks as much as does the labour market.

The point that real property is relatively heterogeneous and
indivisible is obvious and requires no elaboration. But some of its
institutional peculiarities are less obvious and will now be
explained, though without any attempt at the precision of
terminology which would satisfy a lawyer. Although it is
customary to speak of buying or of owning property, the
subjects of transactions are not really land and buildings themselves but 'interests' in property, proprietary rights.

If a man buys the freehold of a house with vacant possession and not subject to a mortgage, it is reasonable to speak of him as buying that house and becoming its owner. In other cases, however, the matter is not so simple. If the man buys the freehold of a house with a sitting tenant who has a lease expiring in 1960, he cannot do what he wants with the house but takes over the obligations incurred by his predecessor in title. Thus what he buys is the right to receive the rent payable by the tenant until 1960, the duty to meet the landlord's obligations for repairs, etc., as laid down in the lease to the tenant and, finally, the right to gain possession of the house and to do what he wants with it in 1960—supposing the tenant to be unprotected by the Rent Acts. In this case there are two interests in the property: that just described, the freehold subject to the lease; and the tenant's interest, the leasehold. This is the right to occupy (or to sub-let) the house subject to the obligation to pay the rent and possibly to keep the interior in good repair. This interest can be transferred, just as can the freehold subject to the lease; if the tenant sells it, he is said to 'assign' it and the assignee takes over the interest. If, on the other hand, the tenant were to sub-let the house, he would not be transferring his interest, he would be creating a new and additional interest in the property, subsidiary to his own.

Occupation leases, that is leases where the lessee occupies land and building, cover a wide field. They may be for a term of as long as forty-two years (multiples of seven are customary), perhaps with a tenant's option to break, i.e. to surrender the lease, at twenty-one years, or they may be weekly tenancies which persist until landlord or tenant gives notice. Leases for up to three years or for no specified term, such as a monthly tenancy, are more properly called Tenancy Agreements; but whatever the period, the lessee can be called a tenant. The rent paid by the tenant is usually a rack rent, a term which does not indicate extortion but simply means that the rent approximates to the full rental value of the land and buildings together. Leases vary in other respects besides their duration, particularly as regards the division of obligations concerning rates, repairs and other outgoings between landlord and tenant. In general, the longer the term of the tenancy the greater are the tenant's obligations. In addition to these obligations a lease may bind the tenant in other ways, for example the tenant of a flat may covenant (agree) not to use the premises for any business purpose.

Building Leases

The other major class of lease is the building lease, a lease with a long term, most frequently ninety-nine years, granted on the condition that a building be erected on the site. The rent reserved under the lease is known as a ground rent.

A simple example will demonstrate the nature of the building lease system. A, the freeholder, grants a ninety-nine year lease of a site to B, a builder, at a ground rent of £100 per annum. B constructs a building of a type agreed with A and sells the lease to C, who lets it to D at a rent of £500 per annum, say for a term of seven years, with D liable for rates and internal repairs. Then there will be three interests in the property:

A, who is called the ground landlord, owns the right to receive £100 per annum ground rent and the 'reversion' of the property, that is the right to possession of the whole property, land and building, at the expiry of the building lease.

C owns the right to receive £500 per annum rack rent from D during the currency of D's lease and possession thereafter. He has to pay £100 ground rent to A and to deliver up the property in good repair at the expiry of the building lease. He is liable for all outgoings on the property except for the rates and the internal repairs which D has covenanted to undertake.

D owns the right to occupy the property until his lease expires, subject to the obligation to pay £500 per annum to C, to pay rates and to undertake internal repairs.

It is evident that it would be misleading to say that A 'owns' the land and C the building, for land and building are not separable.

Before granting the lease, being then freeholder in possession, *A* did own the land, but now he owns the interest described above: a first charge on the property and the reversion.

This example is a particularly simple case, and in practice all sorts of permutations are used. There is some regional variation in the customary method of procedure, and in many areas of Britain building leases are rarely used, all land for development being sold freehold. Where the system is used, a fourth interest in addition to the three listed above is frequently created. Suppose, for example, that *A* grants a lease of a large area not to *B*, the builder, but to *F*, who divides up the area, constructs roads and sewers and then leases one part of the area to *B*. In this case a leasehold ground rent, sometimes called an improved ground rent, is owned by *F*. *F* receives £100 per annum leasehold ground rent from *C* and pays, say, £70 per annum to *A*. The difference of £30 per annum is *F*'s profit and interest for dividing the land and providing roads. The property will revert to *F* only a short while before it reverts to *A*; his interest, the leasehold ground rent, is a terminable interest and his reversion is nominal.

In cases which are more complicated than the one described, the ground rent reserved under a building lease frequently bears no particular relation to the value of the site at the time of construction. Two identical houses side by side built by the same builder at the same time may bear very different ground rents. It is not necessary here to explain this possibility by giving a detailed account of the complexities of the leasehold system[1]; two examples will suffice. A lease may be granted for a capital sum in addition to a ground rent, so that the latter is less than the full value of the site. Or though the total of ground rents on an estate may represent the value of the land leased, they may be apportioned unevenly between the various properties so that some bear a high ground rent and others a low or even nominal ground rent (a peppercorn rent).

[1] For a useful exposition see C. H. Sargant, *Urban Rating*, Ch. II, or A. W. Fox, *The Rating of Land Values*, Ch. II.

Valuable Consideration

There is frequently no simple relationship between the nature of an interest and the method of payment when that interest is the subject of a pecuniary transaction. With the great majority of leases a rent, a periodic payment, is part of the valuable consideration paid by the lessee. But very often the valuable consideration will consist of an initial capital payment (a premium or fine) in addition, except where the duration of the tenancy is not known in advance. Thus with a weekly tenancy agreement, which remains in force until either party gives notice, the value of the interest acquired by the tenant is indeterminate and he will be prepared to pay a premium only if he has reason to believe that he will have some security of tenure and thus regards his interest as having a longer term than it appears to have. Premia were paid to the landlords of rent-controlled accommodation because once in possession the tenants had security of tenure and could not be turned out at a week's notice even when they held under weekly tenancy agreements.

When a freehold changes hands, the purchaser may pay a single sum to the vendor. But this is not always the case; the purchaser may instead pay an annual charge in perpetuity, a 'rent charge'. Or if the purchaser takes the freehold subject to a mortgage granted by the vendor he is in effect combining an initial capital sum, the cash payment, with a periodic payment, the interest and repayment on the mortgage.

In many cases, therefore, various combinations of capital payment and periodic payment are possible. No doubt custom rather than bargaining founded upon detailed calculations often determines the combination adopted, but this will not always be the case. Since, in any event, customs tend to fade away if they become inconvenient, it is worth while to indicate the factors which determine the optimal combination.

One factor is the interest rate. If the purchaser's marginal opportunity rate of interest is higher than the vendor's, he will be prepared to offer a higher increase in periodic payment to offset a given reduction in the initial payment than the vendor will require to compensate himself for that reduction. The substitution of an intermediate amount of increase in the periodic payment for the given reduction in initial payment will therefore be mutually beneficial. It will pay both parties to continue such substitution of instalment for premium until either their marginal opportunity rates are equal or the whole payment is periodic. Building leases, for example, where the whole payment is periodic probably owed their popularity partly to landowners having a lower opportunity rate of interest than builders. This was not the only factor, but it must have played a part, since at least in the latter part of the nineteenth century landowners frequently helped to finance the construction of houses by the builders to whom they granted leases.

The tax structure can also play a part in a number of ways too complex to rehearse here. If, for example, instalments but not premia were allowed as tax-deductible expenses, this, by itself, would lead purchasers to prefer payment by instalment.

Lastly, since the reliability of the purchaser's promise to pay instalments is of importance to the vendor, he will be prepared to accept a smaller increment of instalment in substitution for a given decrease of premium from a financially solid purchaser than from a small or unknown concern. It is for exactly the same reason that the freehold of a shop let, say, to Woolworth's or Boots will sell for more than if it were let on exactly the same terms to an independent shopkeeper whose 'covenant to pay' means less. Similarly, well-known multiples sometimes obtain a lease even when their rental bid was not the highest; they are known as good tenants who are practically certain never to fail to meet their obligations.

In the rest of this book the point that payment may be a combination of premium and instalment is not continually repeated as a qualification, and the analysis is expressed in terms of rents and prices. Thus Chapter V is concerned with the prices of the freehold of farms sold with vacant possession, of farms sold with a sitting tenant and the rents paid by tenants under occupation leases or tenancy agreements.

B

CHAPTER II

URBAN PROPERTY VALUES

The Determinants of Prices

TO start with, it is convenient to assume that everyone in the property market is well informed regarding asking prices and interests in property available for sale. This assumption will be dropped later, as will the further assumption that everyone is always prepared to engage in any property transactions which can be expected to yield at least a small gain, pecuniary or non-pecuniary.

Let a person's (or firm's) Ceiling price for a particular interest be defined as the maximum he would be prepared to pay for that interest; it will be different for different persons. Let the owner's Floor price for a particular interest be defined as the minimum sum for which he would be prepared to sell that interest. Then it follows from the assumptions made in the last paragraph that a particular interest will be sold if one or more persons have a Ceiling price greater than the Floor price. The excess of Ceiling price over Floor price means that both parties will gain from the transaction, and the two assumptions imply that they will know this and will act upon it. If only one person has a Ceiling price in excess of the owner's Floor price, the price realized will be somewhere in between. If there are more than two persons prepared to offer a sum acceptable to the owner, the price must lie between the two highest Ceiling prices, since the purchaser will have to outbid his rivals.

What determines a purchaser's Ceiling price for a particular interest? In the case of a purchaser who is an investor and buys the interest for the income he expects to receive from it, his Ceiling price will equal the present value to him of the anticipated

8

net income discounted at a rate of interest equal to the yield obtainable on alternative investments with similar characteristics. This rate of interest will thus reflect not only the riskiness of the investment, the expected duration of the income and so on, but also the price at which alternative investment interests can be acquired. The present value of the interest to the purchaser consequently reflects the attraction of investment in alternative properties.

This will not always be the case with the purchaser of an occupation interest, so his Ceiling price may sometimes be less than the present value to him of the interest in question. Suppose, for example, that at his opportunity rate of interest the present value to A of the right to occupy a particular property for twenty-one years is £5,000. He may nevertheless not be prepared to pay this much if he can get a 'better buy' elsewhere. Thus if the alternative has the same present value but is obtainable for £4,500, he clearly will not be prepared to pay more than £4,500 for this one. In order to cover such cases, Ceiling price cannot simply be said to equal present value to the prospective purchaser. Ceiling price must equal this or, if it be less, the price at which any substitute interest can be bought (plus the difference, if any, between the present values of the two interests).

Similarly, the Floor price of an owner will equal the present value to him of his interest or, if it be less, the cost of equivalent reinstatement. This is the price for which a substitute interest can be obtained, plus an allowance for the cost and bother of moving, plus the difference between the present values to him of the two interests. In the case of investors as distinct from occupiers, Floor prices are simply equal to present values since these reflect the yield obtainable from alternatives.

Prices realized depend upon Ceiling and Floor prices, and these depend upon present values, both of the interests sold and (in the case of occupation interests) of alternatives. Thus the analysis now requires an examination of the determinants of present value. Only a very general statement can be made, because different people will value the same interest differently. The present value to a particular person of a particular interest is the present value of the net returns he expects to derive from its ownership. The relevant rate of interest for Ceiling price is either the rate at which the potential buyer would have to borrow to buy the interest, plus an allowance proportionate to the degree of uncertainty, or the yield he could obtain by investing his own capital in some other way, with an equal degree of uncertainty. Similarly, the rate of interest relevant to Floor price depends on what the owner would do with the proceeds if he did sell the interest.

The receipts which are relevant to net return in any particular case will include the rent obtainable. In the case of an occupier we would count the rent he would be prepared to pay rather than go without the property, thus including in the analysis those cases where the return from property is non-pecuniary. A further item on the receipts side, which will be important in the case of developers and speculators who do not intend to retain ownership for long, is the price the interest is expected to realize when subsequently resold.

The costs relevant in any particular case may include maintenance, the provision of services, rates and depreciation, though this is usually provided for only in the case of a terminable interest. A further item may be the cost of improving, extending or reconstructing buildings. In the case of a bare site this is obviously the major item, and it deserves further consideration.

Given other cost items and the demand for the services of the building, we may conceive of a schedule of expected average net annual returns per pound of outlay on construction. Average and marginal net returns per annum as a percentage of this outlay are shown in Diagram I, which, for the sake of simplicity, does not show any initial stage of increasing returns and supposes an infinite number of possible development plans so that continuous curves can be drawn. It should be noted that since money sums are measured horizontally and percentages vertically, an area represents only a fraction of a horizontal distance. $OADE$, for instance, is OA per cent of OE.

The optimum outlay will be that at which marginal net returns equal the rate of interest. Thus it will be OE if the rate of interest is OA. The capital value of the property when erected will be the present value of the annual net returns ($OBCE$ capitalized at OA), and subtracting the cost of the building (OE) from this

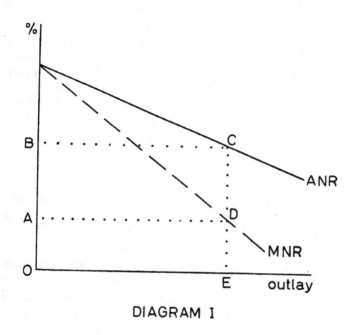

DIAGRAM 1

gives the Ceiling price for the site as a residual. In terms of annual value, the return from the building will be $OBCE$ and the interest charge will be $OADE$, so the difference—$ABCD$—is the rent at which the prospective developer just expects to break even, and is thus his Ceiling rent. This assumes that the builder's profit is included in the cost of construction, and that the developer's profit is included in the opportunity interest cost of his capital. Thus if he acquires the site at a rent below $ABCD$ and if his expectations concerning the net return prove correct, he will reap 'supernormal' profits. It should be noted that the net returns curves relate to magnitudes estimated for the future, so both they and the relevant rate of interest will differ between different potential buyers.

A developer's Ceiling price for the site will be lowered by a rise in the rate of interest or by credit restriction which reduces the amount he can finance to less than OE. A fall in the rents he expects to receive from the building (or the price at which he expects to sell it) and a rise in construction costs will both lower the net returns curves. In either of these cases the optimal construction outlay will fall along with Ceiling price. If nonetheless the developer obtains the site and puts up a building, it will therefore be smaller or less durable than it would have been in the absence of the change in circumstances.

The Determinants of Ceiling Price

It is now time to drop the simplifying assumptions made above and to carry the discussion of present value a stage further by considering some examples.

A simple case is offered by the decision as to what price can be offered for a freehold ground rent with a very distant reversion. This really differs from Consols as an investment only in risk and marketability if the reversion is ignored. Thus the price offered (rate of return required) will be bigger (lower) the better is the cover for the ground rent, i.e. the bigger the ratio of rack rental value to the ground rent and the more reliable the ground lessee. Since ground rents are less liquid and slightly less safe than gilt-edged, most investors will require a return some ½ to 1 per cent higher, and as the trouble of dealing with a ground rent does not vary much with the size of the rent, a lower rate of return will be accepted on a large one than on a small one. The effect of risk on the return required is illustrated by the fact that Scots feu rents fetch a higher price than freehold ground rents because it is felt that there is a possibility that compulsory leasehold enfranchisement[1] might be introduced, with terms unfavourable to owners of freehold ground rents.

A second example is afforded by the Ceiling price of a family for the freehold with possession of a house. What most people do is to choose the best house available within the price range they feel they can afford, without any explicit calculations of present value. This, however, does not invalidate the present analysis as the theory does not purport to be a general description of behaviour. If a family decides to acquire a house for £3,500 rather than another for £3,900, we can say that they act *as if* the present value of the former were more than £3,500 and not more than £400 less than the present value of the more expensive house. With a house, as with an interest acquired as an investment, the lower are the prices at which an alternative can be acquired, the lower will be the Ceiling price.

As a third example we may consider the Ceiling rent offered for a lease of a shop by a retailer. Its present value is the discounted value of the expected stream of receipts minus costs over the length of the lease. These receipts and costs are not independent of one another, since the turnover of the shop is partly dependent upon the way the shop is fitted out, the variety of stock carried and so on. Thus within limits turnover can be increased by incurring greater expenditure. Profit maximization implies that the stream of costs chosen will be that which is expected to lead to the revenue stream giving a maximum to the present value of the shop.

This example is worth pursuing further, in order to show that the actual procedures followed lead to results consistent with the above theoretical statement. Now, the impossibility in practice of making any precise estimate of future cost and revenue streams is due to two kinds of uncertainty. Firstly, future conditions can only be vaguely guessed at. In consequence, most men will try to estimate only the annual revenue and cost they may reasonably

---

[1] A right of ground lessees to buy out the freeholder. Feu rents are perpetual and the owner is thus really only the holder of an irredeemable mortgage.

expect at present, and will bear in mind any obvious prospect of future increases or decreases. Secondly, uncertainty exists in that even at present, let alone in the future, the effect on revenue of such cost changes as, for example, hiring an extra sales clerk or installing a new counter cannot be ascertained. Thus the combination of inputs which will maximize profit cannot be nicely worked out, and the potential purchaser may assume (he has no basis for assuming anything else) that the most profitable way to run the shop will be the same as with other similar shops. He can therefore base his calculations on the gross profit margin, the selling-force requirement for any given turnover, and other data relating to similar shops of the same type unless some obvious difference is expected. For example, a chain grocery contemplating the acquisition of a shop in a working-class shopping street, where price competition is keen, may use the cost experience of their other shops of similar size, but allow for a slightly lower gross profit margin.

It follows that the only practicable method for a person to estimate the value of a shop to himself or his firm is to start by estimating the turnover which can be obtained if the shop is run in the normal manner. The gross profit margin, again, will be taken to be the customary one in the trade, and given the size of the shop as well as its expected turnover the various cost items can be forecast fairly accurately by reference to the experience of other similar shops. Thus rental value can be ascertained residually (and capitalized to obtain a capital value if purchase rather than a lease is in question).

It is evident that some procedure of this sort is in fact followed by chain-store organizations, which possess the necessary experience and expertize. It may be done too by the professional advisers of organizations or individuals who lack that experience and expertize. Furthermore, a person who is considering the purchase of a going concern will often be furnished with figures of past results. For example, the advertisements for small shops often make such statements as: 'net takings, £9, 10s. per week, could easily be increased by remaining open on Saturday afternoons'. It can therefore be assumed that the rent offered for a shop is equal to or less than the sum which would be obtained by estimating turnover and then working down to rent as a residual.[1] Even if only a fraction of the people in the market act this way, it seems legitimate and fruitful to assume that *all* of them act *as if* they did.

The process of estimating the possible turnover from a shop is a matter of hunch and experience rather than of scientific method. Such relevant matters as the number of competitors, the population served by the shopping area and its income level will be taken into account; some firms make a count of the number of pedestrians passing the shop.

Finally, the purchase of a vacant freehold site for erection of an office building provides a case where the concept of the average and marginal net returns on building is important. It will be illustrated with an American example dating from the late 'twenties. The table shows construction costs for a skyscraper in New York to be built in the Grand Central area on a site two hundred feet by four hundred and five feet.[2] Allowance has been made for the setbacks of upper storeys from the frontage lines required by the city building ordinances, and for more elaborate interior finish in the higher buildings. The behaviour of the marginal rate of return as building outlay rises is the result of several forces. The main one is that successive increases in the number of storeys produce smaller successive increments in the number of lettable square feet. One reason for this is the setbacks above a certain height required by American law; the other reason is the increase in the horizontal area taken up by corridors,

---

[1] At least one large multiple uses such calculations only to check that its bid is not too high. This firm has the rule of never acquiring a shop at a price such that it could not be immediately disposed of again without a loss. Thus its bid is based mainly on an estimate of the current market value of the shop. However, it is only such large firms as this (whose reliability as tenants is unquestioned) which can obtain a lease even though their bid was not the highest.

[2] Taken from a review by Klaber of Clark and Kingston, *The Skyscraper*, in the *Journal of Land and Public Utility Economics* (August 1930).

No. of Storeys	Construction Cost	Gross Income	Operating Expenses, Taxes and Depreciation	Net Income	Average Rate of Return on Construction Cost	Rate of Return on Increment
	$000	$000	$000	$000	%	%
8	4,891	1,819	885	934	19·1	
15	7,531	2,780	1,169	1,611	21·4	25·6
22	9,644	3,483	1,369	2,114	21·9	23·9
30	12,258	4,181	1,611	2,570	21·0	17·5
37	14,451	4,755	1,795	2,960	20·5	17·8
50	17,398	5,581	2,047	3,534	20·3	19·5
63	20,520	6,302	2,292	4,010	19·6	15·3
75	24,006	6,901	2,590	4,311	18·0	8·6

lobbies, lift shafts and stairs as height increases. Above a certain point the rental value per square foot of office space may rise, however, because of better light and freedom from street noise.

It is tempting to calculate the Ceiling price for the skyscraper site as a function of the marginal cost of funds to a prospective buyer. The exercise would not be useful, however, since there is no reason to suppose that the marginal and average interest rates will be the same (as was assumed in Diagram I). A large part of the expenditure might be financed by a fixed interest loan at a low rate of interest, and the rate of return required by the developer on his equity would then depend partly upon the proportion raised on loan since this is one of the factors determining the risk he bears. It should be noted that since marginal and average rates depend upon the total investment involved (site cost and construction outlay together) the marginal cost of funds cannot be represented as a function solely of construction outlay. This means that the simple diagrammatic analysis of the determination of Ceiling price for a site can only be used if the purchaser's supply curve of funds is infinitely elastic (at OA per cent in Diagram I).

A fall in the rate of interest the purchaser has to pay to borrow and in the yield he could obtain elsewhere on his own funds will both raise his Ceiling price for the site and increase the optimal outlay, making a bigger or more durable building profitable. A fall in the price at which he can obtain the site may also raise the optimal outlay since it reduces the total investment of funds and may therefore lower his marginal interest rate. But apart from this minor and indirect effect via the marginal cost of funds, the price at which the site can be obtained has no effect upon the sort of building which it is most profitable to erect given unchanged average and marginal net returns upon construction outlay. It is therefore misleading to speak of land values as determining the kind of buildings put up; the causation is the other way round: rents and construction costs determine the shape of the average and marginal net returns curves of Diagram I and these, together with interest rates and the availability of funds, determine present values and therefore Ceiling and Floor prices. A rise in the rents of office accommodation in a business area, for example, will both raise the outlay on new buildings there and raise the prices paid for sites for office buildings. This rise in land values is a consequence, not a cause.

The example of a skyscraper being American, a word may be in order about the most profitable height of building in Britain. Here it is rarely profitable to build more than three or four storeys high outside the City of London, the dock area of Liverpool and the commercial areas of Birmingham, Glasgow and Manchester. Costs go up sharply at this height because of the necessity of lifts, though there is some offset to this in the fact that rental value does not decline much with height in a building with lifts, while it does so in a building without them.

'Banks, building societies and insurance offices always demand ground-floor premises; shops will sometimes take first-floor space for showrooms if it is offered with ground-floor accommodation as a single unit; maisonettes built over shops . . . provide three storeys on an economic basis in some areas; but the demand for office accommodation falls steeply with every step that must be climbed. In a town where the ground floor commands a rent of 30s. a square foot, the first floor will yield little more than 10s. and the second floor less than 5s. The cost of construction per cubic foot, on the other hand, goes up by something like ten per cent per floor as the height of the building rises up to the fourth floor; at the fifth the need for lifts, more steelwork and possibly piling raises it much higher. Above that level, if the site area is adequate, the extra cost of each succeeding floor is about the same—it may even decline in a long block served by lifts at each end only—until the twelfth floor is reached; thereafter it mounts again.'[1]

The unprofitability, in English provincial towns, of building high was revealed in an illuminating manner in Plymouth, where a lessee demanded a reduction in ground rent upon being required by the planning authorities to provide an extra storey for architectural effect.[2]

The Degree of Determinateness of Prices

The assumption was made earlier in this chapter that property transactions are made whenever a gain is to be obtained. This requires an extremely well-informed property market and rests upon the further condition that the prospect of even a small gain is both necessary and sufficient to induce a transaction. But although in principle every property owner has a Floor price (who would not sell his house for £50,000?) and everyone has a Ceiling price for any property (who would not buy a farm for £12?), the bulk of actual transactions takes place between people who have decided to sell their property anyway, because, say, they have decided to move or go out of business, and people who

---

[1] From 'Commercial Centres for the New Towns' by the Local Government Correspondent, *Manchester Guardian* (April 5th, 1954). The preceding paragraph is based on information contained in this article.

[2] *The Economics of Central Area Redevelopment.* Report by the Research Committee of the Town Planning Institute.

have decided to acquire property and are looking for something suitable. This is clear in the case of residential accommodation; few households move solely in order to make a capital gain or to save rent. Other transactions will be considered in a moment, but first we must examine the determinacy of prices in the extreme case, in a market where decisions to dispose of property and decisions to acquire property are not made primarily in order to save or gain money by the transaction. Under such conditions, the Ceiling prices for any particular property depend upon the prices at which alternative properties are available. Since the different potential purchasers of a particular property will to some extent consider the same alternatives, the spread in their Ceiling prices for the property in question will not be large. Moreover, the price which the vendor will accept from any one potential purchaser will be conditioned by what he could get from the others. Thus the vendor can fix his asking price, which may be far in excess of his Floor price, by reference to the asking prices of similar properties which are up for sale and the prices recently paid on others which have been sold.[1] In practice many vendors and purchasers, being inexpert in property dealing, will rely on the professional advice of an estate agent or valuer, and conclude their transactions by bargaining in the neighbourhood of the valuation of their adviser.

It follows that in the case of properties for which there are substitutes, the price which will be realized is determinate within fairly narrow limits, and can be forecast fairly well by an expert. What cannot be forecast is the length of time which must elapse until a satisfactory sale is made. If the vendor is forced to sell in a hurry, being in need of cash and unable to borrow, he may have to accept a price well below the market value of his property. Otherwise he may wait a long time before lowering his asking

---

[1] The discussion is in terms of price, but can be rephrased in terms of rent for the case of occupation leases. In many areas the nominal asking price for a house is several hundred pounds above what the vendor expects to get, but since this is generally known it does not affect the argument in the text.

price, since new buyers are coming into the market continuously.

For similar reasons, buyers who are not in immediate need of a property may prefer to wait for a suitable property to be put up for sale rather than raise their Ceiling prices. Thus a chain store which has decided to establish a branch in a particular shopping centre will not immediately rush in and acquire a shop. Instead it will inform local estate agents of its requirements, wait until a suitable shop becomes vacant and then make an offer.

The conclusions of this discussion are that in the case of types of property for which there is a large market and where many of the buyers and sellers are prepared and able to wait to achieve a purchase or sale:

1. Prices are fairly determinate.
2. Prices offered and asked will change sluggishly in response to changes in underlying conditions, since such changes are difficult to distinguish from temporary changes.
3. On the average, some time will elapse between the decision to sell and the date of sale. Thus (in the case of property for occupation) a certain proportion of the property would normally be vacant even if legal formalities and moving[1] took no time at all.

Any further discussion along these lines cannot be usefully undertaken in general terms. Thus property acquisition for investment rather than for occupation is more a matter of price, and to a greater extent is done by experts. However, something must be said about transactions where either the buyer or the seller had not made any previous decision to buy or sell primarily on non-pecuniary grounds. Compulsory acquisition by a local authority or statutory undertaker obviously leaves a seller no choice, and the amount paid him in compensation is regulated by law. But an owner may be asked to sell his property in a voluntary transaction by someone who has a special need for it. For example,

---

[1] These two factors only account for vacancy between the time of agreement to purchase and the time when the purchaser takes possession.

a firm wishing to expand a factory horizontally will want to acquire adjacent property, or the owner of several adjacent buildings may wish to acquire further neighbouring buildings in order to carry out a large-scale redevelopment. In such cases the 'special purchaser' will often have a much higher Ceiling price than any other possible buyer, while the Floor price of the owner, if he be in occupation, will include a considerable amount in excess of present value simply to compensate him for the cost and bother of vacating property he had not intended to vacate. Thus the price paid, if agreement be reached, will often exceed the prices paid for comparable properties where there is no special purchaser. Furthermore, since the seller may be aware of the special position of the would-be purchaser, he will ask a high price and bargain hard, so that the price reached is determinate (in terms of our analysis) only within a big range.

Value of the Whole and of the Parts

It was explained in the previous chapter that it is interests in property rather than properties themselves which are the subjects of transactions in the property market. The question therefore arises, where there are several interests in a particular property, of the relation between the sum of their market values and the market value which would attach to the unencumbered freehold with vacant possession. Since we may speak loosely of the value of the whole property where only this one interest in it exists, the problem can be restated as the relation between the value of the parts and the value of the whole.

If the sum of the values of the separate interests were less than the value of the unencumbered freehold, there is obviously a gain to be had by bringing all the interests into one ownership, thus in effect abolishing them and creating that freehold. But if one of the interests is patently not going to come on the market, the market value of the others will not reflect the value of union. Rent-restricted tenancies are the clearest instance of this; the value of the freehold subject to the tenancy reflects only the net income obtained by the landlord and is worth far less than the value with vacant possession since controlled rents are mostly very low. On the other hand, the tenancy itself is not legally assignable, so has no market value (unless tenants can nominate their successors and take an illegal premium for doing so). Thus the sum of the market values of the two interests, assuming only these two to exist, is much less than the value of the whole.

While the impossibility of unifying the ownership of several interests may therefore keep the sum of their separate values below the value of the whole, it is always possible to split the whole. The owner of an unencumbered freehold can sell it subject to a lease to himself, mortgage it or lease it for occupation. Its value therefore cannot fall short of the sum of the values of the most profitable combinations of interests he can create in it by any significant amount.

It is, of course, very frequently profitable to dispose of a property 'in parts', for example by letting on a long lease and then selling the freehold subject to the lease. Indeed, where one building is designed for several occupiers there must be several interests unless the occupiers jointly own the freehold. But the more general reason for a multiplicity of interests is that people vary in their views about the future, their asset preferences and in the amount of capital they own or can borrow. (It is exactly the same factor that explains why governments find it worth while to create several different sorts of paper instead of issuing a homogeneous National Debt.) If, for example, a would-be occupier has a higher opportunity rate of interest or is more pessimistic about the future value of a property than an investor, it will pay the present owner of the freehold to grant a lease to the would-be occupier and sell the freehold subject to the lease to the investor rather than to sell the freehold with possession to the occupier.

Quite apart from any division of interests, it has frequently been supposed that the value of the whole can be divided another way, namely between the value of the land and the value of the building. This supposed 'physical' division of value into site and building value has no analytical value, and is meaningless except in long-run stationary equilibrium.[1] As it has been the subject of some confusion, it requires brief examination.

The following magnitudes can be ascertained or estimated:

T = the market value of a building on a site,

R = the replacement cost of the building,

T' = the market value the property would have if the building on it were new and represented the highest and best (most profitable) use of the site,

C = the cost of constructing such a building (OE in Diagram I),

$S = T' - C$, market value of the site (capital value of $ABCD$ in Diagram I).

If S exceeds T by more than the cost of demolition (net of scrap value), it will pay to demolish the building. Thus it might be said that T could be divided into S and $(T-S)$ the value of the building, since if $(T-S)$ is positive it represents the sum which would just compensate the owner for removal of the building. Nobody, however, will ever offer to pay $(T-S)$, so it is not in any sense a 'market' value.

Alternatively, it might be said that T could be divided between R, the value of the building, and $(T-R)$, the value of the site. But R may be irrelevant to any proposed action, so cannot be called a 'market' value. Thus neither method of division has any useful meaning except in the event of their coincidence, when:

$$S = T - R$$

which requires that:

$$T' - C = T - R$$

Apart from coincidence, the only general case where this equality

---

[1] In order to secure rules of assessment for property taxation which are both simple to apply and capable of precise formulation an artificial distinction may be used, as in most American cities. The 'building value' is often a rough estimate of cost less depreciation according to some rule of thumb. The other part of the assessed value—'site value'—is then made comparable for different properties, which has the advantage that it can be seen whether the relative assessments of different properties appear equitable.

C

is fulfilled seems to be where the existing building is that representing the highest and best use (so that $T=T'$) and is new (so that $C=R$). But then the division is useless since one can simply speak of S, site value, C, construction cost, and T, market value of the property. T will equal $S+C$ in a competitive market, if developer's profit is included in C.

The two divisions will thus be consistent only in long-run stationary equilibrium. But since building value is defined residually and since its equality with R only follows from the assumption that there is equilibrium, the concept is useless for economic analysis. Since no ordinary building is ever sold floating in the air, this is not surprising.

CHAPTER III

THE NATURE OF THE URBAN
PROPERTY MARKET

Market Imperfections

THE last chapter examined the determination of the prices and
rents paid for individual interests in property, and it is now time
to turn to their general level and movements in that level. It was
argued above that in the case of such types of property as houses
and offices the price which any particular interest will fetch is
determinate within fairly narrow limits. It must be realized, however, that the argument applies only to those types of property
in which there is a fairly large volume of transactions. Furthermore, it requires that buyers and sellers, lessees and lessors, be
well informed about the situation. Where these conditions are not
fulfilled, the relative skill in bargaining of the two parties and their
knowledge will play a considerable part in determining prices.
Consequently the transactions made, even if they were publicly
recorded, would only afford a rough and ready guide to the movements of availability, credit conditions, building costs and all the
other factors which determine property values. In other words,
the forces susceptible of economic analysis determine only the
broader features of the situation. This will be so to a higher
degree the more transactions are veiled in secrecy, the smaller is
the number of transactions and the more heterogeneous are the
properties concerned. On all three counts the amount of relevant
information will be less, and the last two counts make a smaller
number of alternatives open to the parties. Thus, to name but one
obvious example, particularly large vacant sites in central areas are
not readily comparable unless they have very similar situations.

    Lack of information is an important cause of imperfection not only with regard to current prices and rents but also as concerns state intervention. As will be argued in a later chapter, planning controls create a great deal of uncertainty. Furthermore, legal complexities and taxation rules can be such that property owners who are not experts and who do not take expert advice may be unaware of some of the possibilities open to them.

The Long Period

Another feature of the property market which makes analysis difficult is the slowness with which rents and prices respond to changes in demand conditions. One reason for this is that it is difficult to perceive such changes. A rise in vacancies in a particular area may be the result of some chance factor or may reflect a permanent fall in demand. In the latter case it may be some time before rents or prices begin to fall, since unless the change is apparent to each individual landlord, landlords may not lower their Floor rents until a long wait convinces them that they can no longer let their vacant accommodation at the rents formerly obtained. The degree of sluggishness so caused will of course vary between different kinds of property, being least where owners are best informed and where the supply is relatively homogeneous.

A movement towards an equilibrium position may also take place very slowly because only a small fraction of property interests come on the market in any one year. Consider, for example, a shopping street where all the shops are occupied by tenants on twenty-one year leases. In the extreme case, if these were spread evenly over time only five per cent of them (approximately) would come up for renewal in any one year. Consequently, if the allocation of shops between different trades is significantly different from the equilibrium one, the rents on new leases may exceed an equilibrium level for some years. To show this let it be supposed that there is a given number of shops in existence, that they are exactly similar and that the only traders who can occupy them are grocers and milliners. In Diagram II the total number of shops is *AD*, of which *AC* are at present occupied by grocers and *CD* by milliners. D_G is the grocers' demand curve for shops and D_M is the milliners' demand curve, their demand being measured leftward from *D*. The curves are

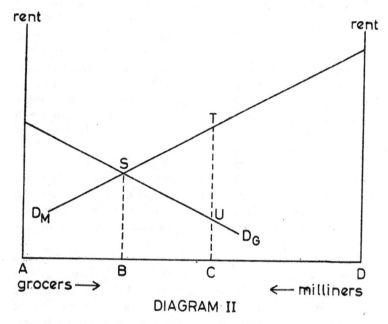

DIAGRAM II

downward sloping for two reasons; firstly, in any given situation some traders will be more optimistic or efficient than others; secondly, because turnover and hence the capacity to pay rent is assumed to fall as the number of competitors increases.[1] The position of the curves is shown on the assumption that millinery

---

[1] This is not always true. Shops of a particular type may be clustered either because they are attracted to a certain location or because a cluster attracts more customers than the same number of shops would do if scattered. The second-hand bookshops of Charing Cross Road, London, afford an example. But since not all the shops there are bookshops it can be concluded that the number will increase and/or that the curve does not slope upwards for the whole of its length.

turnover, and hence milliners' demand for shops, has been expanding rapidly relatively to grocery sales, so that equilibrium would require only AB grocers and the transformation into milliners of BC grocery shops.

If a few leases now come up for renewal, and the market is fairly competitive, the new rents will lie around the level of TC, considerably in excess of the equilibrium level BS. Only as grocers' leases expire will milliners take over grocery shops and the level of rents on new leases begin to fall towards BS. This process may take considerable time. Thus, as a result of an increase in demand the rents currently agreed may rise by more than the equilibrium level has risen. In other words, rents are to be explained less in terms of equilibrium analysis than with reference to the absence of equilibrium.

The process would work much faster if some grocers were prepared to assign their leases at a profit to milliners. The value of his shop to the marginal grocer is only CU, and he can sell his lease for a sum equalling the present value of TC less the rent under the lease for the number of years unexpired. The greater the number of grocers prepared to seize this opportunity, the quicker will equilibrium be reached, and the less significant is the argument of the previous paragraph. But in practice, as was pointed out in the last chapter, the owners of occupation interests in property are frequently uninterested in the possibility of disposing of them in order to make a capital profit. Many traders feel that their business is trading, not property dealing, and may even be unaware of the possibilities. Family businesses in particular often choose to carry on in the old way for as long as they can, so that when they own the freehold or a very long lease their shop will not come on the market until death or retirement ends the business.

Shop Rents

The factors determining the relative market values of similar interests clearly depend upon the type of property involved, and to go any further beyond the principle that they depend upon different net revenue streams the argument must be confined to a particular market. As an example, consider the relative rents of the shops within a particular shopping street.

Two main factors determining the turnover and hence the rental value of any shop in a given location are the flow and character of pedestrian traffic past the shop during shop hours, and the number of competitors. These in turn depend on the general pattern, location and importance of the shopping centre in which the shop in question stands. In general, turnover will be greater the larger is the number of shoppers passing the shop. It is because of this that a position next door to a bank is inferior to one where both neighbours are other shops; since banks close early, have no window displays and no illuminations they attract no pedestrian traffic in the late afternoon or evening. Similarly, it is a disadvantage to be next to a cinema as it is shut in the morning, attracting no traffic, while later on it may create queues which, constituting an obstruction, may actually repel traffic. On the other hand, a bus stop which does not have this latter effect can be beneficial to turnover.

Given the traffic flow and the position of competing and complementary shops, the value of a shop is affected by its size and shape. In general, value increases with depth, but less than proportionately. The frontage of the typical suburban shop is about eighteen feet, and a frontage smaller than, say, fifteen feet is less valuable per front foot. In a shopping centre where turnover is typically bigger for any type of shop, the standard frontage is between twenty-five and thirty feet, but small speciality shops can use smaller frontages while certain shops (particularly in large shopping centres) require much bigger frontages. In such centres space is in any case so valuable that almost any frontage can be used. Thus a popular-priced women's dress shop would probably have an optimum size of thirty feet by eighty feet, yet a frontage as narrow as twenty-four feet could be used (at some extra cost) by constructing an arcade entrance to provide enough window space. Frontage space is important nowadays, primarily because it gives display space, and much less because it gives light; the widening of a shop may increase turnover. Of course, the importance of display space varies according to the type of shop; bakers, for example, have relatively little need for it.

Because corner shops provide a greater display area and because in many cases they are passed by two streams of pedestrian traffic, in the larger shopping centres they are normally worth more than nearby shops of equal size. This does not mean, however, that all types of shopkeeper will bid more for a corner shop. Fish shops, for example, do not need the extra space for display, and a corner is a positive disadvantage with the ordinary open type of fish shop. Again some shops require a rectangle with shelves, racks or cupboards along the sides so that the cashier or manager has clear vision of the whole shop. A side street window takes up space on one side, either reducing interior width or causing the shop to dispense with storage space along that side. On the other hand, even though display is unimportant, small corner sites are particularly valuable to tobacconists if both of the streets have a heavy volume of pedestrian traffic.

Among other factors which affect the value of a shop are whether it has rear access for delivery, good storage facilities and so on.

The bargaining between shopkeeper and landlord relates not only to rent but also to the term of the lease. Normally, the term is some multiple of seven years. Leases of thirty-five or forty-two years without any options to break on either side are now common in the case of shops in first-class positions taken by the better known multiples. In the really cream positions and, in general, when rents are expected to rise, landlords may prefer a shorter lease. The tenant, on the other hand, would generally want a long lease in order to give him security of tenure, with options on his part to break at seven and fourteen years when he is not sure that the position is a good one.[1] In trades where the

[1] At present, however, shop tenants have considerable security of tenure under the Landlord and Tenant Act, 1954.

life of shop equipment is determined more by physical depreciation (e.g. fish, grocery) than by obsolescence (e.g. women's
gowns), a high cost of shopfitting causes tenants to desire a lease
of at least twenty-one years.

In the case of some types of shop, special requirements in the
way of expensive shopfitting and/or a particular kind of building
may make it preferable to build a new shop rather than lease an
existing one unless a particularly long lease can be obtained.
Examples of this are furnished by Marks and Spencer and a large
self-service grocery. Apart from this, the question of owning
shops versus leasing them is largely a matter of the availability
and price of capital to the individual firm as compared with the
rate of interest at which the market is currently capitalizing
occupied shop property. It is rare, however, for the owner of a
particular shop who is putting it on the market to offer it for
either sale or lease, so the choice between the purchase or lease
of any particular shop is not always open to the shopkeeper.

Movements in Rents and Prices

Investment interests in property, that is interests whose owner
is not an occupier of the property, are not essentially different
from stocks and shares from the point of view of investors,
except that they are in general less liquid. There is no central
organized market resembling the Stock Exchange for mortgages,
freehold ground rents and the freeholds or leaseholds of tenanted
property. There are therefore no quoted prices; transactions
involve personal negotiation and the parties get in touch through
lawyers, estate agents or by personal contact, often advertising
their requirements. Since purchase involves borrowing or for-
going the acquisition of alternative investments, however, the
yield on investment interests in property is linked to the yields
of securities quoted on the Stock Exchange. Indeed, the two sets
of yields tend to move broadly parallel to one another, the two
types of investment being broad substitutes. It is true for both
of them that the pattern of yields depends upon differences in

risk, expectations of future net income, differences in tax treatment and similar factors.

It follows that analysis of the general level of yields on real property investments is part of the theory of interest. Certain *ceteris paribus* propositions can therefore be laid down without further ado. Firstly, a secular growth in the National Debt relative to total income from real property will lower the returns on real property relatively to gilt-edged rates. Secondly, an increase in the quantity of money relatively to money national income will lower the rate of return on real property investments. Thirdly, actual or prospective anti-landlord legislation will raise the yield on interests in real property. These propositions follow from the fact that a diminution in the relative quantity or attractiveness of an asset will raise its yield compared to the yield on substitute assets. A fourth proposition also follows; it is that an increased preference on the part of occupiers for owning their accommodation, leading to an increase in the proportion of owner-occupiers, will lower the rate of return on real property. Since purchase involves the sale of other assets or borrowing, the change in preferences has the same effect as a general alteration of asset preferences in favour of real property and against paper assets.

The amount of returns, as distinct from the percentage returns, from investment interests equal the rents and premia paid by occupiers net of the lessors' liabilities. An understanding of the forces which determine the value of occupation interests is therefore necessary to the analysis of investment values. Furthermore, rents and prices with vacant possession are of central interest in urban land economics because they both determine, and are determined by, the allocation of accommodation between competing uses. The next step, therefore, would ideally be a separate examination, for each of the main kinds of property, of the structure of demand, the process by which rents and prices alter, the causes of changes in demand and the factors determining the length of leases. But unfortunately any such systematic exposition is impossible. Very few studies have been made of the behaviour of rents or prices.[1] Consequently all that can be attempted here is to consider two examples of the relation between movements in rents and changes in demand conditions.

Office Rents

The first case is the market for office space in the City of London during the boom which followed the First World War. Before this boom, during the war years, the demand for offices in the City was reduced below its pre-war level, so when tenancies expired they were often renewed at a lower rent; indeed, in some cases landlords allowed reductions in rent where leases were still running. This happened, for example, with a Company owning a very considerable leasehold estate adjoining the Stock Exchange:

'Shortly after the outbreak of war, the Stock Exchange was compulsorily closed, and although after some lapse it was re-opened, practically no business was transacted for a very long period, and such transactions as took place were on a cash basis only. The immediate result of the outbreak of war and the compulsory closing of the Stock Exchange was that practically the whole of the tenants on this Company's Drapers' Garden Estate, large tenants of long standing, as well as small tenants, claimed from the Company very substantial reductions of rent, and in many cases stated that if the reductions, varying up to 50 per cent, were not made they would have to break their agreements and vacate their offices. In view of the circumstances then ruling, it was practically impossible to hold their tenants to their agreements, especially small tenants, and the Company had to make the best arrangement possible under the circumstances, with the result that the rentals from the Drapers' Garden Estate fell from £33,000 to

[1] One reason for this is the extreme difficulty in obtaining the requisite information. Very few usable statistics are published, and records are rarely accessible.

£18,000 per annum, whereas no commensurate reduction could be made in the expenses.'[1]

Tenants whose leases expired during the war mostly refused to renew them, because of the uncertainty of their business situation:

> '. . . tenants found that business was difficult; they did not know what was going to happen, and they preferred to be in a position that they could give up their offices at a quarter's notice or six months' notice. . . .
>
> '. . . when so many young men and . . . more active middle aged men were withdrawn from the City for the service, older men came back, their fathers and grandfathers, to manage these businesses; and they, naturally, would not enter into commitments for leases . . . because they did not know whether their sons were ever coming back to the business. . . .'

A desire of tenants to avoid long-term commitments may be the result either of the expectation of future decreases in rent or, as in the present case, of a shortening of the economic horizon. This was not caused by the diminished demand for accommodation but, like it, was the result of the war. Yet it was the fall in demand which put tenants in a position to get what they wanted. Since there were numerous empty offices, landlords had little choice but to allow tenants to take what was in effect a running option against them. The chairman of a big property-owning company explained it simply:

> 'A man will come and take an office as a yearly tenant; he will then give notice to quit and he will ask you to extend his notice for, say, three months or six months, and we do it. And that is how he keeps on, renewing his notice so that if the market goes down he can clear out, and if it goes up we are in his hands.'

[1] This and other quotations are all taken from the minutes of evidence of the Select Committee of the House of Commons on Business Premises, 1920.

By the Armistice, therefore, many offices were held on short tenancies. Gradually vacancies fell and rents rose, particularly in the winter of 1919-20; the failure of tenants to renew leases during the war now redounded to the landlords' advantage.

The main reason for an increased demand for accommodation was, of course, the general post-war inflation. Provincial and foreign firms sought to establish themselves in London; turnover in the markets of the City rose rapidly so that firms had to expand to at least their pre-war size, and men returned from the services were returning to their old jobs or setting up on their own. Furthermore, there had been no building during the war and premises taken by the Government had not yet been given up. New building in progress actually aggravated the position, since before new offices could be erected old ones had to be demolished. For example, the Port of London Authority had to dispossess everybody on the east side of Seething Lane before work was started on their new building.

Proximity to the markets is of the greatest importance in the City, which is divided into fairly sharply defined zones round the different markets. The importance to many firms of being in the proper district was therefore such as to make the demand for office space very inelastic. It was even said that some businesses, unable to get premises, were leaving the country, and certainly there was no exaggeration in the statement that 'If you go a mile out you may get for £1,000 similar accommodation to that for which we are asked £1,500, but that mile is hopeless for some firms.'

The result of the increased demand was reflected both in rent increases and in the decrease in vacant accommodation. New buildings were let on the plans before the foundations had even been laid, a very big change from pre-war days when 'any tenant had the option of taking up thirty or forty different places'. One big firm owning property had to print a letter of reply to applicants seeking office space, there were so many of them. Sitting tenants received offers of large sums to assign their leases, and some who were fortunate in having leases with several years yet to run sold at very high prices.

Rents rose throughout the City, especially in:

'Two particular districts, the one round the Baltic – Leadenhall Street, St. Mary Axe's and Fenchurch Street. That particular district has increased enormously in value . . . owing to purely commercial causes. Very many large firms have come up from the provinces during . . . or immediately after the war, and the nearer they got to the Baltic the more business they do; . . . competition has been extraordinarily keen. The other district I think you may put as within a very short radius of the Bank of England or the Royal Exchange.

'. . . the Stock Exchange was very busy. It began to absorb more and more offices; that made them scarce in that quarter of the City. Then banks have been particularly busy, and insurance offices, and they have absorbed a very large number of smaller offices and made them into one large office. . . .'

Both direct evidence and the obvious existence of an excess demand for office space indicate, however, that the rents on new lettings and renewals did not rise as much as would have been possible. Evidently not all landlords maximized short-run profits. Thus a tenants' representative distinguished:

'. . . three kinds of landlords at the present time. There are the big landlords who, on the whole, have fairly good relations with their tenants; there are the comparatively poor landlords, of course they are probably not the owners of the highly rented premises; but there is a third class rapidly coming along, the speculative landlord, and syndicates are being formed with a man merely as a figurehead, and I have had instances where these speculative landlords have been very extortionate.'

A representative of one of the first kind of landlords, in denying charges of profiteering, said that they would never have put up rents had not rates (which were nearly always borne by the lessor), and the costs of cleaning and attendance risen a great deal since 1914, but this seems slightly to overstate their aversion to making money. A more ingenious argument was put forward by an insurance broker who was less critical of landlords than other tenant witnesses. He admitted that:

> 'The strong argument of the company in favour of such a big increase was that they were rebuilding on several sites at the ruinous cost of present times, and that if rents fell in, say, ten years to pre-war level the enormous depreciation would mean ruination, and that such depreciation must be met out of the increased rents now obtainable.'

An examination of how landlords behaved towards sitting tenants when the time for renewal came throws some light upon their behaviour. In the case of offices there is no goodwill built up by tenants which would weaken their bargaining power:

> '. . . there might be goodwill in the little island just outside the Royal Exchange, where the insurance brokers are. That is the highest rented spot in the world, just in that one island. There would almost be a goodwill in that little island, but that is all.'

The representative of a big property-owning company said that before the war his company had rarely raised rents, even to yearly tenants who had been in occupation for many years, since they were not out to get the highest rents possible from old tenants. 'I have a great deal of sentiment in me and we have never liked to raise our old tenants more than we have been absolutely obliged.'

These professions did not impress representatives of the tenants, who complained bitterly. The representative of the big company replied by showing that 'We always renew a sitting tenant at a lower figure than we could have got from an outsider', and gave figures for some cases where sitting tenants had declined the company's offer and left:

> 'Messrs. Curwen, of Cannon Street House. Their old rent was £180. They were a firm of many years' standing. We

offered to renew them at £600 and they went and we relet the
offices at £800 a year. Lambert Oswald and Roberts, Suffolk
House. Their old rent was £180. We offered to renew them at
£390, and they declined, and we relet them at £550. Yates,
Suffolk House. The old rent was £90; we offered to let at £250;
he declined, and we relet at £350. Ward, of Cannon Street
House. The old rent was £110; we offered £400; he declined;
we let them at £600. Messrs. Tingle, Comber and Co., of 110
Cannon Street; their old rent was £140; they declined a
renewal at £400, and we relet them at £650.'

Another case quoted was as follows:

'Levy Brothers and Knowles is a case which I particularly
wish to put before you. Their rent was £425. That was let to
them in 1871; that is 50 years ago, for a three or six years'
agreement, and afterwards yearly; so they have been over 40
years a yearly tenant. We offered to renew them at £1,200 a
year; they were very indignant with us, and that is one of the
cases where we told them they would have to reply at short
notice, because there was another tenant in the house who had
signed an agreement for those offices, if they gave them up, at
£2,000 a year. Then they took them at £1,200 a year, and we
told them that they could go and let them at the £2,000 if they
wanted. I only wish to show you that we have not extorted
from them the rent we could have got in the market.'

There is no doubt that landlords knew how much they could let
their properties for if the existing tenant left. An estate agent
explained how:

'In every case that I have had of my own property, I have
been bombarded literally by outsiders, total strangers, who say
they understand that Mr. So-and-so has a short lease and pays
so much rent (you can always find these things out at the
Guildhall from the Rating Valuation List) and so on, and offer
me exorbitant prices if I will turn those tenants out. It is very
difficult in one's client's interest to refuse an offer of a rent of

£1,000 a year from one man, unsolicited when you are only getting £500 for the time being.'

Not all of the excess of the rent obtainable from a new tenant over the offer made to the sitting tenant represented generosity on the part of the landlord, however. Quite apart from long-run considerations, there is the fact that except in the small lettings (of one or two rooms) alterations were nearly always required when a new letting was made: '. . . that is to say that one set of rooms as let to one tenant is not as the succeeding or incoming tenant would choose to have them; and the cost of those repairs on a tenant going in are very heavy.'

What conclusions can be drawn from the above survey? It is evident that landlords and at least those tenants who were in search of accommodation were fairly well informed about rents being currently offered and agreed. Since, in addition, the number of transactions was fairly large, two of the conditions for a flexibly functioning market listed at the beginning of this chapter were satisfied to a considerable extent. On the other hand, office space was far from homogeneous, quite apart from physical differences in buildings, because of the great importance of location. Yet the importance of this factor can be exaggerated since not all types of office user have strong locational preferences, so that many would-be tenants presumably sought premises in several parts of the City. On balance, therefore, we may regard office rents as having been fairly sensitive to changes in demand. Even so, however, the evidence shows that some landlords looked ahead longer than the terms of leases currently being granted, so that the rents they charged were more stable than rents elsewhere. Before the war they frequently renewed leases at an unchanged rent for years on end, and after the war they preferred maintaining the goodwill of their tenants to obtaining still higher, but less secure, rents from new tenants.

While long-term rather than short-term profit maximization reduced the amplitude of some rent changes, a different factor worked in the opposite direction, making rents more flexible than

D

the average terms of leases would appear to allow. On the one hand, when demand was low some landlords granted rent reductions before the expiry of leases. On the other hand, when demand was high some tenants took a capital profit by assigning their leases for large premia. Such adjustments are probably only important in the face of particularly violent fluctuations in demand.

Lastly, it is clear that rent changes are related to the proportion of accommodation which is vacant. It was suggested above that this relation may be a delayed one because it will take time for it to become clear when a change in the vacancy rate is due to an alteration in demand rather than to random factors. With the violent shifts in demand during and after the war, however, this delay was probably much less than usual. Landlords with vacant accommodation lowered their Floor rents and tenants sitting under leases were able to force their landlords to accept reductions in rent. After the war, rents rose and vacancies fell, though the really sharp increase in rents appears not to have come until vacancies were down to an extremely low level.

Housing Rents

The relation between vacancies and movements in rents may be further illustrated by the example of the rent of flats in a large city. A study relating to Stockholm during the inter-war period[1] shows that there was a high positive correlation between the number of vacant flats and the number of 'Flat to Let' advertisements in a major daily newspaper and an equally striking negative correlation between the number of vacancies and the number of 'Flat Wanted' advertisements. This strengthens the view that the vacancy rate is a good indicator of the market situation.

Some complicating factors must be mentioned, however. For one thing, when an agreement expires, the position of the sitting tenant vis-à-vis the landlord is different from that of a potential tenant negotiating for a vacant flat. The sitting tenant is used to

[1] Dickson, 'Hyresförändringar och Bostadsledighet' (*Ekonomisk Tidskrift* March 1947).

the flat, and to move elsewhere would involve both cost and bother. If decoration is a tenant's liability, the cost to the landlord of preparing the flat for a new tenant will be small, while the cost to the tenant of moving might include decoration. Thus, except where vacancies are very high, the position of the landlord is strong, and the sitting tenant may agree to a higher rent than if he were a new tenant.

The variations in the policies of different landlords can be fairly considerable. For example, when vacancies were high in London in the early 'thirties, some owners circulated to agents a list of all their vacant flats, while at least one property company merely indicated that it had a flat to let in a particular block however many were vacant there, and hung curtains in all but one! Some owners may bargain with potential tenants, while others quote the rent on a take-it-or-leave-it basis. An owner who wants a steady return will be careful to arrange his leases so that their expiry is spread out over time. Differences such as these may be reflected in considerable divergence of rent patterns over time. Thus, if vacancies arise, some owners may not reduce rents to attract tenants but choose instead to spend more on advertising and improve the quality of services provided. (Flowers in the lobby and the like make a good impression.) Consequently the movement of the net incomes from different blocks of flats may be more uniform than the movement of rent rolls.

Considerations such as these do not affect the general picture, however. Dickson's study showed that in Greater Stockholm there was a fairly close relationship in the period 1923-41 between the vacancy percentage and the amount and direction of change in average rents from year to year.

'The borderline between the housing reserve which is so large that rents fall and that which is so small that they rise seems as a rule to have lain around a vacancy percentage of one. Up to the end of 1929 the vacancy percentage was less than one and on the whole rents rose up to and including 1930. . . . Then the vacancy percentage grew for three years and average rents sank simultaneously at an increasing rate. The highest vacancy percentage registered, 3·14, occurred at the end of 1932 and the largest rent reductions happened in the following year. In 1937 the vacancy percentage sank back under 1, and thereafter rents began to rise again. . . . (Apart from a minor irregularity in 1925) a deviation from the general scheme did not appear till the years 1940 and 1941, when the rent increase continued although the vacancy percentage lay at over 1·5 at the end of 1939 and 1940. This probably hung together partly with increased costs and partly with expectations of housing shortage and inflation in connection with the war; during 1941 the vacancy percentage sank to 0·43 and since then diminished further.'[1]

Rent control was introduced in 1942.

A slightly different pattern was discovered by some American investigators. They present figures of

'rent and occupancy levels for six cities, covering various years between 1930 and 1938. The similarity in the pattern of movement of the two variables for all cities is quite striking. A period of declining rents and occupancy was succeeded by a period of rising occupancy but stable rents; only after occupancy levels had reached some critical point or zone did further increases in occupancy ratios result in significant rent increases. In almost all of these cities rents were higher at a given occupancy ratio on the downswing than they were at the same occupancy level on the upswing. All this was true despite significant differences in the occupancy level at the critical point and differences in timing of the rent rises. Occupancy levels at the critical point ranged from slightly more than 93 per cent to almost 99 per cent. The first year of rent rise varied between 1935 and 1939.'[2]

---

[1] Dickson, *op. cit.*, pp. 30-1.

[2] Rapkin, Winnick and Blank, *Housing Market Analysis* (Housing and Home Finance Agency, U.S.A.), p. 24. The most interesting part of this work is more conveniently accessible in an article by Blank and Winnick in the *Quarterly Journal of Economics*, Vol. LXVII, 2.

The same authors also consider it likely that the rents of single-family dwellings vary more than those of dwellings in multiple-dwelling buildings, while vacancies fluctuate less. They present a possible explanation which may be summarized as follows. If the landlord of a block of flats reduces the rent he asks for the flats which are vacant, he will sooner or later have to concede reductions to his present tenants. The marginal revenue from letting one more flat is thus below average revenue. If demand falls without any significant change in elasticity, the landlord will therefore accept an increase in vacancies rather than reduce rents. On the other hand, a single-family dwelling must be fully let to produce any income at all, so its landlord will be prepared to accept a very low rent rather than keep it vacant. For this contrast to be valid, leases must on average be of short duration and discrimination between tenants must be impossible. Unfortunately the information required for a direct check on these conditions is not available.

Rent Control

Where rents are controlled or, in the case of public housing, set at a level which leaves an excess demand for accommodation, the price mechanism is not allowed to function. The consequent effects upon the allocation of resources therefore bring into sharp relief the functions of the price mechanism.

Firstly, the price mechanism allocates dwellings between competing users. In its absence, which people occupy which houses is determined by past events; people stay where they are because it is difficult or impossible for them to obtain any other accommodation. In the case of public housing, tenants are chosen by public authorities according to criteria which, in Britain, vary from place to place but which normally give preference to people from the locality. Thus the geographical mobility of labour is reduced. Similarly, the allocation of different types of dwelling within each locality is also sterilized as people whose demand has changed are unable to shift into the type of dwelling they have come to require.

The presence of some uncontrolled housing does not alter these conclusions, since while a move from controlled to uncontrolled accommodation is possible, the increase in rent will be greater (or the decrease less) than it would be in the absence of control.

Secondly, the price mechanism determines the amount of resources devoted to the repair and maintenance of housing. When rents are controlled, such expenditure does not generally have any effect in maintaining the income from tenanted housing as it would in the absence of control. Instead the landlord's income is independent of the amount he spends and he will therefore only have an incentive to spend more than the law requires insofar as he anticipates decontrol. Furthermore, an unchanged rent coupled with a rising cost of repairs and maintenance decreases his ability to make the expenditure. The joint result of these forces is that privately-owned rent-controlled housing will depreciate physically faster than it would in the absence of rent control: demands on the building industry are reduced.

Thirdly, the price mechanism determines the proportion of privately-owned housing which is let and the proportion of that which is let furnished. With rent control and its corollary, security of tenure, landlords are not free to decide between letting unfurnished, letting furnished and selling with vacant possession. When there is no effective control over the latter two, landlords who obtain vacant possession through the death or voluntary departure of a tenant find it much more profitable to let the accommodation furnished or to sell the freehold or a long lease with possession than to relet it at the controlled rent. Consequently the proportion of accommodation which is let furnished and the proportion which is owner-occupied will rise steadily.

The strength of this force can be gauged by comparing the movement of the prices of houses sold with possession with the movement of the prices of houses sold without vacant possession. For example, houses sold with vacant possession in England and

Wales in the first quarter of 1945 fetched a price which, on average, exceeded the 1934-39 level by over 80 per cent. The corresponding figure for houses sold without vacant possession was only 30 per cent.[1]

Fourthly, the price mechanism determines the amount of new housing built by private enterprise. Insofar as the rents and prices of new flats and houses are subject to control, the profitability of new construction may be kept low. But supposing that they are not controlled, the effect of rent restriction on private new building requires consideration of its effect on building costs and on the prices and rents of uncontrolled accommodation, i.e. as compared with what they would have been in the absence of control. As to costs, they will be affected favourably by the reduction in the amount of repair and maintenance work done by the building industry for the owners of rent-controlled property. As to rents and prices, they may be either higher or lower than in the absence of control, as will be shown below.

Fifthly, the price mechanism determines the distribution of real incomes. Rent control obviously shifts this in favour of the tenants of rent-controlled accommodation and against their landlords. In the case of uncontrolled accommodation, however, the net effect may go either way. As pointed out above, rent control may make the value of uncontrolled property either higher or lower than it would have been in the absence of rent control. In the latter case the effect is to alter the distribution of income in favour of the tenants of uncontrolled accommodation as well as in favour of the tenants of controlled accommodation.

In order to examine what determines whether decontrol would raise or lower the values of property at present uncontrolled, let it be supposed that there is no owner occupation. Suppose further

---

[1] *Report of the Interdepartmental Committee on the Selling Price of Houses* (Cmd. 6670), pp. 7 and 9. For an admirable general discussion of the Economics of Rent Restriction see the chapter so titled in *The Post-War Financial Problem* by Professor F. W. Paish, and *Houses to Let* by Geoffrey Howe and Colin Jones, a pamphlet published by the Conservative Political Centre, which refers to various official reports and other discussions.

that the tastes and incomes, and hence the demands for accommodation, of those living in controlled accommodation (call them C) are the same as those of those living in uncontrolled accommodation (call them U). Then if, under control, U are less crowded and live in superior accommodation than C, when rent control is abolished some of C will bid away some accommodation from U. The rents and prices of the accommodation which was not subject to control will therefore rise. Conversely, if U were more crowded and occupied inferior accommodation, the market values of their accommodation will fall.

Suppose, alternatively, that C and U live in accommodation of the same quality and equally crowded but that either U are poorer than C or that their scales of preference give a lower weight to housing. Then the abolition of control will enable some of C to bid some accommodation away from U, raising its market value.

Considerations of various factors one at a time in this manner suggest that a *fall* in the rents and prices of uncontrolled accommodation is more likely to follow the suspension of rent control, *ceteris paribus*:

(a) the richer are U relatively to C;

(b) the higher the place of housing in the tastes of U relative to C;

(c) the more crowded are U relative to C;

(d) the more inferior is the accommodation occupied by U relative to that occupied by C.[1]

---

[1] Since this was written an admirable statistical analysis of the effects of decontrol has been published by A. C. L. Day. See his article 'A forecast on rents: The middle class market' (*Manchester Guardian*, Jan. 8 1957).

CHAPTER IV

THE PATTERN OF URBAN PROPERTY VALUES[1]

Equilibrium Analysis

IF the determinants of the equilibrium constellation of prices and resource-use changed infrequently or slowly, while adjustments to such changes took place relatively rapidly and without much friction, the actual pattern of prices and resource allocation would usually correspond fairly closely to the equilibrium pattern. It would thus be possible to analyse the existing state of affairs in terms of an equilibrium construction. Now so far as the long run is concerned, this is not generally the case with urban property, because the great durability of buildings makes urban change a very slow process and one that is never completed.

If conditions were different and buildings had very short lives, the actual shape and form of a town would be close to its equilibrium pattern. The building on any site would differ but little from the building which it would be most profitable to erect were that site unoccupied. Thus office users would nearly all be accommodated in buildings designed for office use, single-family dwellings would not be split up into flats and, in general, property would be utilized as it was designed to be. But since this is not the case, since most towns are not in equilibrium, it is impossible to present a comparative statics analysis which will explain the layout of towns and the pattern of buildings; the determining background conditions are insufficiently stationary in relation to

[1] On the subject of this chapter see: Richard M. Hurd, *Principles of City Land Values*; Fisher and Fisher, *Urban Real Estate*, Ch. 13 and 14; R. M. Haig, 'Towards an understanding of the Metropolis' (*Quarterly Journal of Economics*, Vol. 40, pp. 402-34).

the durability of buildings. In other words, each town must be examined separately and historically. The features of London, for example, can be fully understood only by investigating its past; it is as it is because it was as it was. Of course, a few matters can be explained in non-historical terms because some of the background conditions have remained unchanged. These are the physical conditions: geology and topography; but they explain only some features and leave a great deal to be dealt with by looking back at the course of development over time.

In the short run, however, an equilibrium analysis in general terms can contribute some understanding. Given the existing standing stock of buildings, the pattern of rents can be analysed by examining demand conditions, as can the pattern of land use insofar as it is flexible—i.e. to the extent that some buildings are capable of more than one use. The point is that the actual rent and use pattern of a given stock of buildings will approach the equilibrium pattern within a period sufficiently short for changes in that stock (by reconstruction and new building) to be negligibly small. It is true that many occupation leases are for a considerable term of years, but since leases can be sold or surrendered by agreement, tenants are not as immobile as this fact might suggest. Thus, as a first approximation, the way in which existing buildings are used and the pattern of market values may be discussed in equilibrium terms.

General Accessibility and the Pattern of Rents

The relative rental values of different buildings which are substitutes in that they are used by the same type of occupier, for example office buildings, depend on three factors. The first is the physical condition of the building: whether it is modern or old, whether it is centrally heated and so on. The second is what may be called its 'general accessibility', its nearness in terms of travel cost rather than distance *per se* to all the other buildings of the town. The third is its 'special accessibility', its nearness to particular complementary facilities. Both these types of accessibility are matters of location, but special accessibility in contrast to general accessibility varies with the type of user. General accessibility is desired by practically all users except hermits; firms like to be accessible to many employers and customers, and most householders like to live centrally. It is true that many householders would choose a suburban house rather than a central flat even if they both cost the same, but the main reason for this is that they want a house and a garden, not that they would dislike living in the middle of a town.

The special accessibility of a property is different for different users. An office in the Covent Garden area has great special accessibility for a fruit merchant but very little for a stockbroker, who needs to be near the Stock Exchange. Many shopkeepers require not only the general accessibility of a main thoroughfare but also the special accessibility of a shopping district. Sellers of medical equipment cluster near Harley Street and legal bookshops near the Law Courts in order to be accessible to their particular customers.

Suppose now that special accessibility is of no importance, so that the preference of a firm or person as between physically similar premises depends only upon their general accessibility. It is thus assumed that what matters is the relation of a property to the street network and the railway system, and that a property is regarded as better situated the easier it is for people and goods to move between it and the rest of the town, while the land-use pattern of a neighbourhood makes no difference to the attractiveness of premises there: everyone wants to be near (accessible) to everyone else in general but not to anyone in particular.

Under these conditions, the general level of rents for each type of accommodation will depend upon the amount of each type of accommodation in relation to the demand for it. But for every type of accommodation the rental value will vary with the degree of accessibility, being highest in those parts of the city which are most central with respect to transport facilities. Those concerns and persons which place the higher value on general accessibility will occupy the more central of the premises suitable for their use, while the more remote premises will be occupied at lower rents (for physically similar accommodation) by those who place a smaller premium on accessibility.

In the short period, which is under consideration here, the geographical distribution of land uses is obviously conditioned by the geographical distribution of the different types of building. But within this framework a definite pattern will tend to appear wherever one type of building is suitable for more than one type of user, as, for example, office accommodation can be used by lawyers and accountants, or shops by different kinds of retailer. Thus if the average lawyer places a higher premium on accessibility than the average accountant, the percentage of office accommodation occupied by lawyers will be higher (and the percentage occupied by accountants will be lower) in the more accessible parts of town than in the less accessible parts, since in equilibrium office rents and hence the differentials according to accessibility must be the same for both lawyers and accountants. Insofar as the composition of the standing stock of buildings permits it, the result is therefore for the use of property to depend upon its accessibility, so that certain types of use are concentrated in the inner rings of the town and others in the outer rings.

Special Accessibility

This is an interesting conclusion, for it demonstrates that a definite pattern of land use will develop in a large town even when special accessibility is unimportant. In other words, the complementarity of certain uses is not a necessary condition for the development of use zones. It is, however, a very important factor and must not be forgotten. Firstly, particular uses are attracted by some uses and repelled by others. Thus, to give but a few examples, a location outside the entertainment district is inappropriate for a new theatre unless it has some special prospective audience; some lawyers need to have offices near the courts of justice; a button maker will seek accommodation near clothing manufacturers; and a position near a glue factory is unsuitable for housing. Secondly, some uses tend to cluster because different firms in the same trade benefit from one another's proximity, as in the case of diamond merchants and antique dealers.

The result of these factors is that the order of preference between locations differs for various classes of user even though all place some value on general accessibility. In consequence the tendencies noted above for a definite land-use pattern to develop are more marked than if general accessibility alone were relevant. Rent levels in certain central areas are markedly higher than the rents of comparable accommodation elsewhere near the centre, the uses so concentrated generally being those types of retailing and financial business which place a particularly high premium both on general accessibility and on proximity to other such businesses.

New Building

This use and rent pattern will cause the nature of the new buildings put up to vary according to the degree of accessibility. Consider the type of new building which is most profitable. In order to make the analysis simple, it is assumed that all sites are of the same size; that special accessibility is unimportant; that there are only two degrees of general accessibility, central and peripheral; and that there are only two types of buildings: offices and warehouses. If now the differential of central rents over peripheral rents is 5s. per square foot of floor space for offices and only 2s. for warehouses, the average net returns curve for office construction will be higher relative to the average net returns curve for warehouse construction on a central site than on a peripheral site. It follows that if construction of both types of building is profitable, the new offices will be built centrally and the new warehouses will be built peripherally. More generally: the higher the degree of accessibility, the greater will be the proportion of new buildings put up which are of types (some of) whose users are willing to pay a high premium for accessibility. The tendency observed above regarding the use of existing buildings is thus powerfully reinforced in the long run. The character of land use in the central parts of towns will be systematically different from the less accessible areas.

Site Values and Building Density

In general, areas where rents are particularly high show a greater building density and have higher site values than the rest of the town. A presumptive explanation can be given as follows.

Consider two sites which are physically identical, A in such a high-rent area, B elsewhere. Because of the difference in rent levels in the two areas and the absence of any major difference in building costs, it can be assumed that the average net returns curve for site A will lie above the average net returns curve for site B for the whole of its length. It follows that the marginal net returns curve for A will probably be higher for the whole of its length, as in Diagram III.[1] Given the same opportunity cost rate of interest, OU, in respect of both sites, the cost of the most profitable building, i.e. the optimal outlay, will be JK greater on the central site, site A. If the type of building erected is the same on both sites, this will mean that the building will be taller and/or have greater site coverage. In general, therefore, the density of new building (and of existing buildings too, if the town is not changing rapidly) will be greater where rent levels are higher.

A similar argument, subject to a similar reservation, indicates that site values will vary with rent levels. In terms of Diagram III the annual value of site A, $VWYU$, is greater than that of site B, $RSTU$. High rents, therefore, make dense building profitable and make sites valuable; it is misleading to reverse this and say that high site values cause building to take place at a high density.

---

[1] This is not necessary—MNR_A could fall below MNR_B for part of its length. Even so, the following argument would be invalid only if the optimal outlay fell within this range. There is no reason to suppose that this case will occur often.

If special accessibility is of no importance, site values will therefore vary with general accessibility, diminishing as the cost of travel to the centre of the town increases (assuming that this cost is proportional to the cost of travelling to all other properties in the town). The geographical pattern of site values will therefore reflect the network of communications, though two factors may make this reflection less than perfect. Firstly, the geology of some sites may make building operations expensive or limit the size of building which it is safe to erect. Secondly, the value per square foot of a site will depend upon its size as well as upon its location

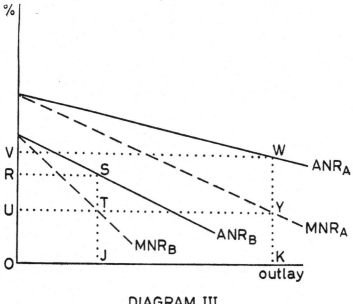

DIAGRAM III

and physical condition. For example, a single site which is large enough for a house or shop but too small for a block of offices or flats will be worth less than the average amount per square foot in an area where most new buildings are large blocks.

Allowance for the importance of special accessibility makes for a much more complicated pattern. A belt of low site values may separate two areas of high site values, even when there is no great difference in general accessibility, if both the surrounding areas contain facilities proximity to which confers advantage. For example, competition for space near a railway station and near a Stock Exchange may leave an intermediate area of lower rents and site values. Thus there can well be more than one area of peak land values.

CHAPTER V

AGRICULTURAL LAND

CUSTOM and legislation both influence the responsiveness of
farm rents to changes in basic economic conditions. This chapter,
however, is concerned only with these latter and the following
analysis mainly relates to the equilibrium level of rents. As a
further simplification it is assumed that agriculture produces only
one product, 'corn', so propositions relating to the output and
price of corn must be taken as referring to indices of agricultural
output and prices.

The Rent of a Single Farm

To start with, it will be assumed that all farms are occupied by
tenants under leases terminable by either landlord or tenant at
twelve months' notice. Landlords provide the farm buildings and
are responsible for the cost of repairs and insurance, so that their
net income equals rent received less repairs, insurance, manage-
ment expenses and any tax such as tithe redemption charge.
Major improvements, such as the construction of a new barn or
drainage works, are undertaken by landlords, while an outgoing
tenant receives or pays compensation for any increase or decrease
in the value of the farm due to his method of working it. Finally,
it is assumed that the outgoing tenant receives compensation and
the incoming tenant pays for the value of tenant right—the
agricultural equivalent of work in progress. By thus supposing
mutually acceptable arrangements to exist, the complex problem
of compensation and tenant right is left out of the picture.

Diagram IV relates to a single farm. The demand curve for its
corn is horizontal, as farmers take price as given. The marginal

cost curve MC (*a*) relates to a particular farmer, (*b*) excludes the opportunity cost of his (and his family's) labour, (*c*) refers to a period sufficiently long for all his costs to be variable and during which good and bad years cancel out. It includes the interest and depreciation on stock and machinery, and because of the indivisibility of machinery, marginal costs may fall up to a certain

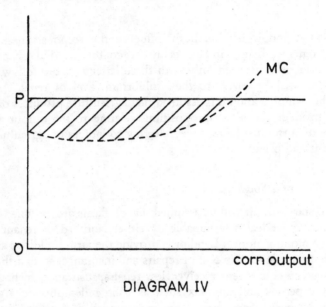

DIAGRAM IV

point.[1] Clearly the height and slope of the curve depend on the nature of the farm and landlord's improvements, factor prices and technique. It is assumed that the farmer's effort is given; a change would shift the MC curve. After a point, marginal costs rise because of diminishing returns as more factors are applied to the farm, not because of rising factor prices as the farmer buys more factors: they are assumed to be in infinitely elastic supply to him.

If the price of corn is OP, the shaded area is the surplus of the

---

[1] In order to keep the diagrams simple, the very high MC of the first few units of output is disregarded and the curve is assumed to be smooth.

value of output over all costs, except rent and the farmer's own labour. Part will go to the landlord as rent, and the rest is the farmer's net income. What determines the division?

The maximum rent the farmer will pay is, disregarding the cost of movement, the surplus less what he could earn elsewhere. If his best alternative is outside agriculture, the latter amount is his potential earnings less (a) the rent he would have to pay for a house if he were not a farmer, and (b) an allowance for differences in non-pecuniary advantages. If, as may be assumed for the moment, his best alternative is as tenant of another farm, his alternative earnings equal the surplus he could earn there less the rent he would have to pay. On the other hand, the minimum rent the landlord will accept is the rent he could obtain from any other would-be tenant of comparable standing, and this depends on the same factors as the offer of the first farmer. Now, if the farmer is much more efficient than all other would-be tenants, he is likely to be much more efficient (produce a bigger surplus) than them on other farms too. This means that his offer for any one farm will not differ much from theirs, even though he is more efficient or hard-working. Consequently, the maximum and the minimium referred to above will be fairly close, and so the rent of farm A will tend to equal the rent of any alternative farm, B, plus the excess of the surplus an average farmer can earn on A over what he can earn on B. Thus, *ceteris paribus*, the equilibrium rent of any farm will be greater the higher are the rents of other farms and the bigger the surplus producible on it. Consequently, differences in rents can be attributed to differences in the surpluses that can be earned by an average farmer; the better farmer will not pay a higher rent, he will earn a higher income.

This argument does not require complete mobility of farmers. Even if no farmer is prepared to move more than twenty miles, there is a chain of competition linking the rents of farms far distant. Thus a fall in rents in the north will tend to lower rents near by, and this process will continue southwards until it reaches the southern end of the country, just as an Olympic torch travels further than any of the runners who carry it.

Differences in Rents

Apart from this complication, differences in rents can be ascribed to two factors. Firstly, there is location. A remote farm will have to incur higher transport costs than a farm near markets, either directly, or indirectly, in the price received for the product and prices paid for factors. In terms of Diagram IV its marginal cost curve will be higher and, if the farmer does not himself pay the cost of transporting his produce to market, the price line will be lower as compared with the farm which is less remote. Its equilibrium rent will therefore be correspondingly lower. Secondly, one farm may yield a higher surplus than another (in the sense defined above) because it is bigger, consists of better land or is better equipped. Whether its superiority is due to the quality of the soil or to improvements is indifferent; given equality in respect of the first and second factors enumerated, it will fetch the higher rent. It should be noted that this does not necessarily mean that the farm with the greater yield per acre will have the higher rent, as can be shown with the aid of Diagram V. Suppose farms *A* and *B* to be equally situated in regard to location and factor prices and to be of equal area. With the cost curves as drawn, farm *A* will fetch the bigger rent though its output (and hence yield per acre) is less than that of farm *B*.

Even under the assumptions made at the beginning of this chapter which imply the absence of legislation giving security of tenure to farmers, rents will respond sluggishly to changes in economic forces. Firstly, farmers are accustomed to changes in income due to weather conditions here or abroad, so in the absence of widespread economic information it will take both them and landlords some time to distinguish the longer-term changes in economic factors which call for a revision of rents. Secondly, actual rents may move more freely than nominal rents, particularly under leases which are not terminable at twelve months' notice. For example, if the trend is downward, occasional abatements of rent or an increase in expenditure on repairs by the landlord may be substituted for revision of the contract. Thus some rent inflexibility is to be expected even in the absence of any non-business relationship between landlord and tenant. If, however, there is some social constraint upon hard bargaining by either party, it will probably not increase the rigidity of all rents equally. The reason is that such constraints are likely to operate more powerfully where there is a sitting tenant, known to the

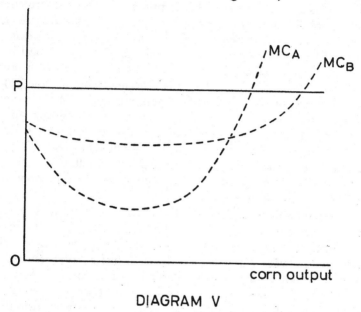

DIAGRAM V

landowner and established in the community, than where there is a change of tenancy. Thus, in a period when the trend of rents is upward, it is to be expected that the rents of farms let to the same tenant year after year will rise more gradually than the rents of farms where one tenant succeeds another.

Capital Value

The price at which a farm with a sitting tenant will sell is the discounted value of expected future net income. It is commonly expressed as a multiple—the number of years' purchase—of the net income currently yielded by the farm. (The net income is the rent received less landlord's expenses.) The most important determinant of the number of years' purchase which an investor will offer is the opportunity cost of capital, that is the rate he could obtain on an alternative investment of equal magnitude and risk. Thus a rise in Stock Exchange prices and a fall in mortgage interest rates will tend to raise the number of years' purchase at which tenant-occupied farms are currently being sold. However, the number of years' purchase will only equal the reciprocal of the opportunity cost rate of interest if certain conditions are fulfilled. They are: (a) no change is expected in net income; (b) income from a farm is treated for taxation purposes in the same way as income from alternative investments, and similarly with the proceeds of sale when estate duty is assessed; (c) there is no expectation of selling the farm later at a different price. If, for example, rents and capital values are expected to fall, the number of years' purchase will be less than the reciprocal of the opportunity cost rate of interest.

The assumption made so far, that all farmers are tenants, may now be dropped in order to consider the price a farm will fetch if offered for sale with vacant possession. The price cannot fall much below what it would be if the farm had a sitting tenant,[1] for the vendor always has the alternative of acquiring a tenant and then selling the farm. On the other hand, the price may rise above this level. It might be argued that there is a mechanism to prevent this, since if a premium on vacant possession develops, occupying owners will sell their farms and move to other farms as tenants in order to make a capital gain. But this is unlikely: the capital gain would have to be very large in order to offset the cost and bother of movement, and few farmers would act in this manner merely to make a capital gain. Thus a premium on vacant possession will arise if (a) sitting tenants have security of tenure and (b) farm rents are below their equilibrium level. The market

---

[1] Plus payment for tenant right, since if the farm is vacant the purchaser acquires this.

for farms is not, as assumed above, such that a man can obtain a tenancy whenever and wherever he wishes, and it hardly ever happens that a man gets a lease by overbidding a sitting tenant. The stickiness of rents means that when their tendency is upward it is difficult to get a farm. Nor will the owners of tenanted farms be able to make a capital gain by evicting their tenants and offering the farms for sale with vacant possession when custom or legislation give security of tenure. Thus it seems that farms sold with vacant possession can fetch considerably more than similar farms with a sitting tenant if tenants have security of tenure.

An investor purchaser will be unlikely to offer more for a farm with vacant possession than for a similar farm already tenanted (since he buys in order to get a tenant) unless it is easier to increase the rent on letting to a new tenant than with a sitting tenant. On the other hand, a farmer purchasing for occupation may well offer more than the capital value of the anticipated landlord's income from similar farms if he is unable to obtain a tenancy on a similar farm. This will be the case if there is an excess demand for tenancies at the ruling rent level, that is if custom or legislation and the natural stickiness of rents make for a rent level below the equilibrium position. In the absence of these conditions, any premium will reflect merely the value of the tenant right which is acquired with an untenanted farm.

Some of these points are illustrated by the following table,

Years	Average Price per Acre		Premium for Vacant Possession
	Vacant Possession	Without Possession	
	£	£	£
1937-39	31·1	23·1	8
1940-42	41·8	28·3	13·5
1943-45	53·7	32·2	21·5
1946-48	81·8	42·3	39·5
1949-51	94·9	45·6	49·3
1952-54	86·8	41·9	44·9

which gives the average price per acre of farms sold since 1937.[1]

When war came, the demand for farms rose, and after a time prices rose. They increased more than rents even in the case of farms with a sitting tenant. This rise in the number of years' purchase appears to have had three roots: the attraction of farm property as a hedge against inflation, the fall in interest rates and an increase in the relative advantages of landed property from the point of view of taxation. The premium for vacant possession rapidly rose above the pre-war average (which represented mainly the value of tenant right), for after 1941 it became impossible for a farmer to obtain a tenancy at all readily: actual rents rose less than equilibrium rents. Because of this stickiness, investor owners could secure a capital gain by selling with vacant possession when a farm became vacant and sitting tenants could outbid investors when their farms were sold, since they could afford to pay an amount proportioned to the equilibrium rent rather than the actual rent. Thus the proportion of farms tenanted fell from 66 per cent in 1941 to about 61·6 per cent in 1950.

Average rents rose by about 13 per cent from 1951 to 1954, so the fall in sale prices, which was mainly due to the rise in interest rates, reduced the premium for vacant possession, though this nevertheless remained substantial.

The General Level of Farm Rents

So far the analysis has related to the rent and capital value of a single farm, given the general level of rents, of farmers' earnings

---

[1] For details and further analysis see: J. T. Ward, 'Changes in the Sale Value of Farm Real Estate in England and Wales 1937-9 to 1951' (*The Farm Economist*, Vol. VII, No. 4); 'Notes and Statistics' (*ibid.*, Vol. VII, No. 6); and an article in *The Westminster Bank Review*, Feb. 1955. A great deal of useful information on rents is given in *The Rent of Agricultural Land in England and Wales 1870-1946*, published in 1949 by the Country Land-owners' Association, which also gives a list of references on agricultural rents.

and of the opportunity cost of capital. In order to examine the determinants of the general level of farm rents it is convenient to simplify the exposition by reverting to the assumption made earlier that all farmers are tenants. The following analysis relates to the equilibrium level of rents, and it must be remembered that the actual level will follow changes in the equilibrium level only with a very considerable time-lag.

The equilibrium level of rents is that level at which the number of entrants to farming would equal the number of retiring farmers[1] (since the demand for farms by farmers moving from one farm to another has no net effect on the general level of rents). This equality requires a certain relationship to rule between the earnings of farmers and their best alternatives outside agriculture. Now, a farmer's earnings equal the surplus (in the sense defined above) which he can earn on a farm less the rent of that farm, while his alternative, his transfer cost, equals what he could earn outside agriculture less the rent he would have to pay for a house and an allowance for differences in non-pecuniary advantages. A change in any of these magnitudes will tend to upset the equality of entry to and retirement from farming and lead to change in the level of rents. *Ceteris paribus*, therefore, rents will tend to rise if: (a) the potential earnings outside agriculture of farmers and would-be farmers decrease; (b) the rent of dwellings other than farmhouses increases, or a housing shortage develops; (c) people come to estimate more highly the non-pecuniary advantages of farming; (d) the surplus producible on most farms increases, whether due to a rise in the price of corn, a fall in factor costs, an increase in productivity or some combination of all three. All economic changes which affect the equilibrium level of rents must work through one of these four channels,[2] the fourth being

[1] Unless the average size of farms is in the process of changing. In an analysis of the really long run the size of farms would have to be included as a dependent variable.

[2] A fifth, minor, determinant is the extent to which would-be tenants possess or can borrow the necessary capital for purchasing tenant right and stocking a farm.

the most important in practice, particularly in the shorter run. It is probable that these factors exert their influence mainly by affecting the inflow of new farmers rather than those already working a farm, though a decline in farmers' earnings might affect retirements.

In order to show the way in which the determinants affect the equilibrium level of rents, the effects of three changes will be briefly analysed. Consider firstly the influence of a rise in the level of national income at home but not abroad due, say, to a domestic investment boom. Corn having a positive income elasticity (since here it represents agricultural products in general), the demand for corn will rise. Thus, unless foreign supply to this country is infinitely elastic, the price of corn will increase. This in itself will tend to increase surpluses and thus raise rents. On the other hand, there will be two influences working in the opposite direction: a rise in non-agricultural earnings and rents, and an upward shift in the cost curves of all farms due to a rise in factor prices caused by the increase in the demand for factors. The latter factors could conceivably outweigh the former (and would do so if foreign supply were infinitely elastic), so that farm rents and domestic corn output would actually fall. But output will rise if price rises more than marginal cost at the initial output level. Unless farmers' transfer earnings rise in a much higher proportion still, the equilibrium level of rents will then increase.

A rise in the supply curve of imported corn will raise the demand for domestic corn without having any direct effect upon costs. Output and the level of rents will both increase, output rising to a greater extent the higher is the elasticity of supply of factors to farming. In Diagram VI the continuous lines show the initial position of an individual farm when the price of corn is OP. In the new situation, when price has risen to OP^1 and the expansion of corn output has raised factor prices and hence marginal cost curves, the position of the farm is shown by the dotted lines. If the elasticity of supply of factors to agriculture were infinite, the cost curve in the new equilibrium would be the same as initially (*MC*), and the surplus and hence rent would be greater still.[1]

The last type of change, the effect of which on rents will be

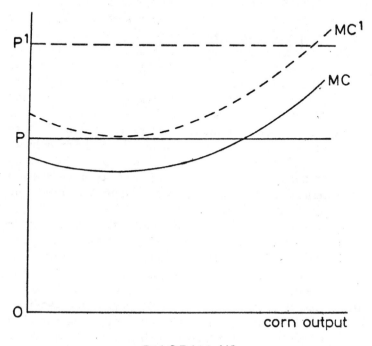

DIAGRAM VI

considered, is technical progress. The discovery of a new technique, implement, etc., will have no effect unless, given all prices, it is profitable to individual farmers to introduce it. If its introduction has no effect on the price of corn, surpluses, and hence rents, will increase. This requires either an infinite elasticity of supply of imported corn, so that the demand for domestic corn is also infinitely elastic, or a zero effect upon marginal cost

[1] By an amount somewhat less than the area between *MC* and *MC¹*, as price would be less than *OP¹*.

at the present output, so that output is unaltered. The most plausible case of this kind is the introduction of a new method of performing some operation which must be done in the same way irrespective of output—a fixed rather than a variable operation.[1] Some methods of disease control, such as sheep dipping, afford simple examples of this type.

Where the elasticity of supply of foreign corn is not infinite, technical improvements other than the kind just mentioned may lead to either an increase or a decrease in output and will lead to a change in price. The rather peculiar case where output may fall and where rents must rise is illustrated in Diagram V, where the marginal cost curve of an individual farm shifts from MC_B to MC_A on the introduction of a new method. If, on the other hand, the curve changes in such a manner as to make an increase in output profitable at the old price, the price of corn will fall and the net result may be a fall in rent, since the price fall may more than offset the reduction in costs.

The effects of improvements upon rents thus depends upon the elasticity of supply of imported corn and upon the type of improvement, and no simple generalization is possible. Attempts to distinguish between improvements which save land and improvements which save other factors of production would add little to the analysis, and in any event they cannot readily be distinguished except upon the assumption of a single product and only one factor other than land. In contrast to the above analysis, therefore, results expressed in terms of such a distinction would not help in understanding rents in a multi-product agriculture.

[1] Thus its cost would be a fixed cost; it would shift only the marginal cost of the earlier units produced, leaving the rest of the MC curve unchanged. The possibility that the improvement might make it profitable to increase the area under cultivation, so raising output and causing a fall in price, is neglected above.

CHAPTER VI

PROPERTY TAXATION—RATES

Nature of the Analysis

RATES, as known in the United Kingdom, are an *ad valorem* tax, the tax base being the net annual value of occupied real property. This is the rent that could be obtained by letting a property from year to year *net* of maintenance and insurance expenses. It is thus the net annual rental value of property gross of depreciation.[1]

The purpose of this chapter, however, is not to discuss current English rating problems. Instead, its aim is to construct a method of analysis which can be applied to particular sets of circumstances. This method has two features which should be noted. The first is that no use is made of the concept of incidence; the treatment is concerned with all the effects of rating without any attempt to collect some of them together under the title of incidence.

The second feature is one of substance rather than terminology; the analysis is a general equilibrium analysis. This means that the question asked cannot simply be 'What are the effects of imposing or raising rates?' It is necessary to specify what is done with the proceeds. To some extent this was done by neo-classical writers in their distinction between onerous and beneficial rates, the latter being those which were spent in providing services from which ratepayers benefited. An alternative is to suppose that the proceeds are used not to increase expenditure but to permit a reduction of other taxes. The following analysis follows this alternative line, though it will be seen that the same approach can be applied to the former class of cases.

[1] For a survey of developments in English rating since 1880 see U. K. Hicks, *British Public Finances*, Ch. IV, and 'The Valuation Tangle' (*Public Administration*, Vol. 32, pp. 229-35).

In order to examine the effects of rates as a substitute for other forms of taxation, it is convenient to suppose that they have not existed hitherto and are now imposed at a uniform rate and on the basis of uniform assessments by local authorities on all occupied property so as to yield £200 million. At the same time, central government grants to local authorities are reduced by £200 million and income tax rates are decreased so as to diminish the yield of personal income taxation by the same amount. Thus the source, but not the total of local authorities' income, is altered and they continue to undertake the same expenditure as before.

In addition to the simplifying assumption that the rate is uniform both as between areas and as between different types of property, three further assumptions will be made—and removed later. Firstly, there are no owner-occupiers: all property is rented; secondly, rates are paid by tenants, not by the landlords; thirdly, there is no rent control.

Effect on Rents

Consider now the effect of the tax changes upon the rents of existing houses and flats. Their occupiers are made worse off by having to pay the part of the £200 million levied on residential property, and better off by paying less in income tax. The exact distribution of this impact effect obviously depends on the degree of progressivity of the tax reduction compared with the pattern of rents in relation to income. Some families will gain on balance and some will lose. But it may be assumed that the net result of this scatter of income effects together with the rise in the price of accommodation relative to other consumer goods and services will be a fall in the demand for accommodation of the great bulk of the population. This means that most occupiers will consider or attempt moving to cheaper accommodation, taking lodgers (or getting someone to share) or securing a reduction in rent. Rents will therefore tend to fall. The same will be true of non-residential space. Faced with rates, many occupiers will consider moving to inferior accommodation or using less space, so some landlords will have to lower their rents in order to keep their tenants. This will force others to reduce rents too, so rents in general will move downward.

As rents fall, net annual values will fall too. In the absence of any substantial change in the stock of buildings at succeeding rating revaluations of property, the rate poundage will therefore have to be increased in order to maintain the total revenue from rates at £200 million. Income tax rates will also have to be raised in order to prevent the revenue of the central government from falling,[1] since the fall in rents constitutes a reduction in landlords' incomes.

Equilibrium will be reached when rents have fallen by amounts equal to the rates, so that the aggregate of rents is £200 million less than before. In this position landlords' incomes are therefore also £200 million less than before, while other incomes are unchanged (including business incomes, since the fall in rents paid by businesses is offset by the rates they now pay). On the other hand, the yield of income tax is also £200 million less than before, so total incomes after tax are unchanged. The distribution of the total will be altered, however. In particular, landlords will receive less and tenants more. Furthermore, all tenants will not be better off to the same extent. Consequently there may be some change in the pattern of demand for accommodation. But apart from this minor effect, the new situation is an equilibrium one, since income, the amount paid for accommodation and the prices of other goods and services are all the same as in the initial position.[2]

This analysis is, of course, a static one. The downward move-

---

[1] This assumes, as seems correct, that rental income multiplied by its marginal rate of tax exceeds the sum of those rents and rates which are deductible expenses for income tax multiplied by the marginal rate of tax on those incomes from which rent and rates are deductible expenses. If this condition were not fulfilled, a general fall in rents would (at given tax rates) *raise* government revenue.

[2] Various other minor effects of the tax changes such as their effect on the incentive to work are neglected, so this equivalence of the new and the old equilibrium is only approximate.

ment of rents towards the equilibrium position will take time, since in many cases leases may have some years unexpired. But even if conditions remain unchanged in all relevant respects, the movement towards equilibrium may be impeded by another kind of 'friction'; rents will be sticky downwards when tenants are in a weak bargaining position relative to landlords. This state of affairs can result if some of the following conditions are fulfilled:

(a) The cost and bother to the tenant of moving, including the disturbance to trade in the case of businesses, are considerable.

(b) It is difficult and expensive for the tenant to secure alternative accommodation.

(c) The proportion of the tenant's total outlay going in rent is small.

(d) The landlord can find another tenant (though at a lower rent) quickly, so that loss of rent through vacancy is small.

(e) The costs which the landlord must incur upon getting another tenant, such as redecorating the premises, are small.

It is likely that there will be some differences between different classes of property in respect of the extent to which these conditions are fulfilled. In declining areas, (b), (d) and (e) will be much less important than in expanding areas, so rents will fall more. Conditions (b) and (d) are more likely to be fulfilled in the case of small houses than of large houses, as the occupiers of large houses can move into smaller houses, so rents of the larger houses will fall most. Lastly, conditions (a), (b) and (c) apply differently to offices, shops and factories; probably office rents will fall most and the factory rents of industries using large fixed equipment least.

Effect on Building

So far in the argument the stock of buildings has been taken to be constant. The next step in the analysis is to consider the effects of the tax change upon the amount and type of new building. As the rents of existing buildings fall or are expected to fall, the rents to be earned from new buildings will also fall. Now, since the rents of agricultural land suitable for development and existing buildings suitable for redevelopment must fall along with other rents, the acquisition cost of sites for new buildings will fall too—assuming unchanged interest rates. It follows that if construction and maintenance costs were to fall in the same proportion, the profitability of new construction would be the same as before rates were imposed, since the gross return from new projects, construction costs, current costs and site costs would stand in much the same relationship to one another as initially.

Construction costs will not fall in the same proportion as rents, however, since the elasticity of supply of factors to the building industry is considerable. Consequently the profitability of new building (and rebuilding) will be reduced and the volume of building will fall. This means both that fewer sites will be developed or redeveloped and that the value of building work per site will fall, i.e. the sites which are built on will be developed less intensively. The fall in the amount of building will, in the long run, raise the level of rents above what it would have been without the tax change.

The point that the effect of the tax change will be to increase the 'land intensity' of new building (i.e. decrease the 'building intensity') can be demonstrated with the aid of Diagram I: a downward shift in the average and marginal net returns curves will diminish the optimum outlay on a given site. Perhaps a numerical example will make the point clearer. The example shows the effect upon the value for development of a freehold site of a fall in rents.

Consider a site with 220 feet frontage, 200 feet deep, in the inner residential area of a large city. Two alternative schemes are possible:

A. The erection of four modern detached 2-storey houses with garages. Suppose (unrealistically) that they are to be let and that in the absence of rates they would fetch £360 per annum each, a total rent of £1,440.

F

B. The erection of a block of 20 flats, each with a garage at the back; a more intensive development. Suppose that, in the absence of rates, they would fetch a total rent of £250 per annum each, £5,000 in total.

The table shows that the value of the site is greater for scheme *B* in the absence of rates, it being worth £8,800 as against only £5,200 for scheme *A*, the less intensive development.

	A		B	
	No Rates	*With Rates*	*No Rates*	*With Rates*
Rent plus Rates . .	1,440	1,440	5,000	5,000
Less: Rates at 5s. . . .	—	240	—	800
Gives: Rent	1,440	1,200	5,000	4,200
Less: Repairs and Insurance .	240	240	1,000	1,000
Gives: Rateable Value . .	1,200	960	4,000	3,200
Capitalized in perpetuity at . .	6%	6%	7%	7%
Gives: Freehold Value . .	20,000	16,000	57,200	45,760
Less: Cost of Construction .	13,200	13,200	44,000	44,000
Fees, etc. . . .	1,200	1,200	2,000	2,000
Interest on Cost during Construction . .	400	400	2,400	2,400
Gives: Value of the Site for Development . .	5,200	1,200	8,800	−2,640

Suppose now that rates are introduced at five shillings in the pound on the rent net of repairs and insurance, and that the total amount which people are prepared to pay for the accommodation is unchanged. The rents obtainable then fall by an amount such that the sum of rent and rates equals the rent obtainable in the absence of rates. The result is, as the table shows, that the profitability of both schemes is reduced. But the reduction is greater in the scheme with the greater building intensity so that now the less intensive scheme, *A*, is the more profitable.

The decline in building will tend to have a multiplier effect, lowering the level of real national income. If corrective action is undertaken by the Government, there will nonetheless be some reduction in the amount of building unless the measures stimulate only building. Thus, if interest rates are lowered, this will partly offset the fall in the profitability of building, but cannot offset it wholly, since even if total investment is restored to its previous level, building must be less than before by the amount by which other kinds of investment are stimulated by the reduction in interest rates.

Some Complicating Factors

The conclusions so far reached are that while the standing stock of buildings remains unchanged the tax change will tend to reduce rents by the amount of rates. This will reduce the volume of building and raise its 'land intensity', so the long-run effect will be that rents rise gradually as the reduction in the amount of building takes effect.

A more detailed analysis must take into account various complications, and some will now be introduced by way of example. One such complication is that different types of property may be rated differently. In order to show the sort of effects resulting from this, assume that agricultural land is not subject to rates while all other types of property are uniformly assessed and rated. The introduction of rates will then, as discussed above, cause all rents to move downward except for agricultural rents. Consequently, assuming no change in interest rates, the acquisition cost of agricultural land for building will not fall along with the acquisition cost of other land. The profitability of building upon agricultural land will thus fall more sharply than the profitability of other building, and relatively more new building than before will be in non-agricultural areas. The long-run effect will therefore be for the rent level of accommodation in non-agricultural areas to fall relatively as the stock of buildings there expands relative to the stock in agricultural areas. The exemption of agricultural land thus tends to check urban growth into the surrounding countryside.

The assumption was made above that rates are always paid by the occupier. Where this is not the case, the imposition of rates will initially make landlords worse off, instead of tenants, and the landlords will endeavour to raise rents as and when leases expire in order to recoup themselves. Since the rents of alternative accommodation will be declining, however, landlords will not succeed to any great extent except where they are in a particularly strong bargaining position. If this type of friction is unimportant, the rents of this accommodation will tend to retain parity with the rent plus rates of accommodation where the tenant pays rates. Apart from the transition period, therefore, it makes little difference whether landlords or tenants pay rates; in either case the new equilibrium position is one where the amount paid for accommodation in rent and rates is the same as before, rents falling by the amount of the newly introduced rates.

The rate of tax—the rate of poundage—may not be uniform over the whole country. If rates are higher in area A than in area B, rents must fall more in A than in B, whether or not accommodation in the two areas is non-competing. The fall in the amount of new building will therefore be greater in A; indeed, the amount of new building may actually rise in B if the building industry is mobile between the two areas and the reduction in the total amount of new building lowers building costs. Whether or not this happens, however, the long-run effect will probably be to increase the stock of rateable property in B relative to A so that if there is no change in the amount each area raises in rates, the initial disparity in rate poundage will gradually be accentuated. There is thus a two-way causation: declining areas have particularly heavy rates, and heavy rates contribute to the decline of an area.

When rent control exists, and is effective in the sense that there is an excess demand for accommodation, occupiers will pay the rates (unless rents plus rates exceed the rents which would rule in the absence of control). This is true even where the rates are paid by landlords, for rent control legislation usually enables landlords in such cases to raise rents by the amount of the rates. In the case of rent-controlled property, therefore, tenants pay less income tax but have to pay rates; landlords' incomes before tax are unchanged. Nevertheless, given constant interest rates, there will be some fall in the capital value of rent-controlled properties insofar as it is expected that vacant possession may be obtained or that rent control may be abolished in the foreseeable future. This fall will not affect the amount of new building, however, for that is determined by the rents net of rates that can be obtained on new houses and flats. The previous part of the analysis applies to such rents unless they too are controlled.

Lastly, the assumption that there are no owner-occupiers can be removed. When the tax change is introduced, some owner-occupiers will wish to avoid paying the whole amount of rates on their present property by selling it or letting it and moving to smaller or inferior accommodation. People and firms in the market for property will also diminish their requirements. In the absence of friction, therefore, the price of properties with vacant possession will fall. But since (assuming no rent control) properties can be either sold or leased, the fall in capital values must correspond to the fall in rents. Thus prices will fall with rents, though, as discussed above, 'friction' may cause different types of property to fall in value in different proportions, particularly since the cost of selling one property and acquiring another is considerable.

CHAPTER VII

PROPERTY TAXATION—THE RATING OF SITE VALUES

The Problem

THE taxation of site values means that the tax levied in respect of each property is proportioned to the value of the site rather than to the value of the whole property as it stands. Such taxation has been frequently proposed in Britain during the last seventy years, both to provide an additional source of revenue and to relieve the burden of the present rates. A variety of arguments have been marshalled in its favour on moral, financial and economic grounds. The moral arguments follow the lines that land values are socially created and that increments in land values are unearned and therefore undeserved. The financial arguments have been important implicitly if not explicitly, for local authorities searching for new sources of revenue have advocated the rating of site values and adopted some of the moral and economic arguments. The most important economic arguments put forward have been that, in contrast to the present English rating system, site value rating would not discourage building and improvements and that it would not lead to undeveloped land being kept off the market in the expectation of future rises in value instead of being made available at a reasonable price.

This chapter is concerned only with the economic arguments. The question considered is what the effects would be of partially or totally substituting site value rating for the rating of annual value. As in the previous chapter, it will be assumed that under the present system all property is uniformly assessed and rated on annual rental value and that the substitution is made in such a way that total revenue and the expenditure of the taxing authorities is maintained at a constant level.

Before beginning theoretical analysis, however, something must be said about the practicability of site value rating and the form it might take. Its advocates have frequently suggested that the existence of site value taxation overseas demonstrates its practicability in Britain. The matter is not as simple as this, however, because the system of long building leases which is prevalent in some parts of the United Kingdom is not used elsewhere, and the complexities of the system are relevant to the problem. Furthermore, the compensation and betterment system at present in force under the Town and Country Planning Acts raises some difficulties in valuing sites of which notice must be taken. It is therefore necessary to consider the liability to site value rate and the tax base; two matters on which a great variety of proposals have been put forward.[1] The discussion runs in terms of the leasehold system, for what is practicable there is *a fortiori* practicable when there are no long leases.

Liability to Site Value Rate

Some schemes propose that all the owners of interests in a property should pay site value rate, each in proportion to the amount of site value enjoyed by him, site value being understood to mean the market value the property would possess if any existing building were razed.[2] Now an imputation of site value between the different interests would be meaningful if the total

[1] For a survey of the various committees which have reported on site value rating and of proposed legislation, see 'Historical Summary', Chapter II of the report *The Rating of Site Values* (H.M.S.O. 1952). Appendix III provides a brief survey of the rating of site values abroad. The bulk of the report is written with particular reference to the system of development charges, now abolished, and is therefore of less general interest than some of the earlier reports mentioned in the 'Historical Summary'. There is a minority report in favour of rating site values.

[2] Valuation is discussed below; the above definition will suffice for the present.

value of the property (*a*) could be divided into site value and building value and (*b*) equalled the sum of the values of the separate interests. It has been shown in Chapter II that condition (*a*) is not normally fulfilled on any independent definition of building value and that condition (*b*) is not always fulfilled either.[1] Basically, the point is that a lessor receiving rent from a lessee and perhaps paying rent to the owner of a superior interest from whom he or his predecessor took a lease, cannot be said to own any share in what the value of the site would be now if it were cleared. If *A* granted a ninety-nine years' building lease in 1880 at a ground rent of £40 per annum, *A*'s successor cannot be said to own the site or part of it: he owns the right to £40 per annum until 1979 plus the reversion of the property in that year. The ground rent of £40 per annum need bear no particular relationship whatsoever either to the value the site would have now if cleared, or to what its value was in 1880, for the ground rent reserved on the property in 1880 may have included interest on money advanced to the builder, or have been made low then in consideration for payment of a capital sum.[2]

Nonetheless, it would of course be possible for the liability to

---

[1] Suppose that if the property were freehold with vacant possession the most profitable course would be to demolish it and construct a new building. In this case, total value equals site value *less* the cost of demolition. But if someone holds a lease on the property with only a few years to run, the value of his interest contains no element due to the possibility of rebuilding and the value of superior interests only reflects such value discounted back from the date when the lease is to expire. Thus in this case the sum of the market values of the separate interests will actually be less than site value! (Of course, the owner of one interest would do well if he could buy up the other interests at their market value. This fact, however, does not alter the point at issue.)

[2] The references given in footnote 1 in Chapter I explain the wide variety of circumstances in which the ground rent reserved in a building lease may differ from the annual value of the site.

Where a lease has more than about seventy years to run, the futurity of the reversion renders it insignificant. From the point of view of the lessee the ground rent is then simply a first charge on the property, much as mortgage interest would be.

pay site value rate to be apportioned among the owners of the separate interests in a property according to some arbitrary rule.[1] Now, as was argued in the previous chapter, it makes relatively little difference whether rates are paid by the occupier or by his immediate landlord, since most occupation leases are of relatively short duration. The serious question, and the one which has been the subject of most controversy, is the division of the site value rate between the owners of interests superior to that of the occupier. A good deal of the discussion has concerned the equity or inequity of this as regards contracts made previous to the introduction of site value rating, but this aspect of it is not considered here.

The aspect that must be considered is the effect on new contracts. Once the site value rate was introduced, the outgoings of owners of interests in property would be altered by every revaluation and by each change in the rate poundage. There would therefore be no interests in real property (other than mortgages[2]) which yielded their owners a fixed money income, and ground rents would lose their attraction for that large class of investors which is prepared to pay a high price for a fixed income which is well secured. Similarly, the uncertainty of the income from intermediate interests would be increased. The cost of funds for new building would thus rise as investors would require a higher rate of return than before to compensate for the increased uncertainty (unless all financing could be done by mortgages).

An analogy will make this effect clearer. Suppose that part of the profits tax of a firm were deducted from the interest upon debentures and the payments to preference shareholders. The incomes of their owners would then vary with changes in the amount of profits and the rate of profits tax and so new deben-

[1] For a description and comparison of two such proposed rules see Sections VI to VIII of the 'Separate Report on Urban Rating and Site Values' (*Royal Commission on Local Taxation*, Final Report (Cd. 638, 1901)).

[2] Unless these were also liable to a share of the site value rate.

tures and preference shares could only be issued if they promised a higher yield than formerly. This would check investment even if money could be borrowed on mortgage as before.

Similarly, the effect of the division of the site value rate would be to reduce the amount of new construction, other things remaining the same. On the assumption that this would be considered undesirable it will therefore be supposed that the site value rate would all be paid by the parties who pay the rates under the present system, i.e. the occupiers or, where rates have been compounded,[1] their immediate landlords. This means that the substitution, in part or in whole, of a site value rate for the present rate would redistribute the burden between properties but not between the owners of the different interests in each property. The same people would be liable to pay rates in either case.

The Tax Base

The second aspect of the practicability of different schemes to be discussed here is the assessment of site value. Some schemes of site value taxation involve the assessment of an annual value; others require assessment in terms of capital values. Which of these alternatives is chosen makes very little difference. The value of any interest can be expressed indifferently either as a capital sum or in terms of an annual payment, the relation between the two depending on current interest rates. The real question, however, is not whether value is expressed as a lump sum or as a rent. What matters is the nature of the interest in the site: is it to be assumed to be of limited duration?

It has been suggested that the imaginary interest to be valued should be of limited duration so that it includes no prospect of any future increases in returns from development for which the site is not yet ripe. Thus agricultural land with a building potential would be valued as agricultural land only, without any element of development value. This is what the proponents of annual

[1] In the case of some flats, offices and houses of low rateable value.

value want to do. On the other hand, the proponents of capital value wish to tax the owner of the land on a basis in excess of its agricultural value and including future building value. In effect, therefore, they require the interest to be of long duration.

Whatever the moral arguments may be, only the second course seems practicable in the case of urban land. The reason is that no developer will normally lease an urban site for a short term of years; he will either take a lease of at least eighty years or acquire the freehold. Thus the value of an urban site for a short term would be very notional indeed. It will be assumed here that sites are rated on the capital value of the freehold.

Each property must of course be valued as though any buildings or structures did not exist on it but all other properties were in their existing state. (To value on the assumption that all buildings and structures were demolished would be impossible, for, as was shown in Chapter IV, the value of any property depends not only upon its general accessibility but also upon the character of neighbouring property.)

Furthermore, in the case of farms, the value of tenant right would have to be excluded. It would be much more difficult to exclude the value of improvements to the land itself, such as drainage. Thus in the extreme case of land reclaimed from the sea it would hardly be practicable to value the land in the state it would be were there no sea wall! But the exclusion of the value of improvements is of importance only in respect of future improvements, since the point is that it is desirable to avoid reducing the incentive to undertake new improvements. This might possibly be done by subtracting from the value of a site (for a period of, say, thirty years) the cost of any improvements undertaken since the introduction of the site value rate and paid for by the owner of any interest in the property assessed. Such deductions would cover not only the cost of improvements on agricultural land but also, for example, the cost of providing roads and sewers on a new building estate. However, the legal feasibility of this device is not certain and it will be supposed here that improved site value is assessed to the site value rate without any deduction for the cost of improvements.

It is generally proposed that sites should be valued as though they were unencumbered. It would be anomalous to assess two identical properties differently because one was mortgaged. Further, it is proposed that no account should be taken of any restrictive covenants imposed in any lease at present held in respect of the property, since the basis of assessment is what the site would be worth if made available for development *de novo*. On the other hand, regard would have to be paid to the existence of easements such as right of light and right of support. It is of course true that it would be very difficult for valuers to obtain details of such rights, but against this it has been argued that a party aggrieved by over-assessment of his property due to neglect of an easement could secure an appropriate reduction in the assessment. The valuing authority could then make an appropriate increase in the assessment of the site benefiting from the easement (the 'dominant tenement').

There are two methods of estimating site value.[1] The first is the 'comparative' method, where the estimate is formed on the basis of information about the price fetched by bare sites of comparable nature. This obviously requires that capacity for judgement which marks the expert valuer. The second is the 'residual' method, where the cost of building and developer's profit are subtracted from the value which it is estimated would be possessed by the building most suitable to the site. The range of judgement required here is very large. In particular, this is so where the most suitable building would be bigger than, or different from, the existing building.

In many such cases there is an additional source of uncertainty: if the property is compulsorily acquired or if planning permission is not granted for the form of development which is most profit-

---

[1] Neglecting the procedure of deducting 'the value of the building' from the total value of the property. Some valuers maintain that this procedure is meaningful, but the fact that they can express the right answer in these terms proves nothing.

able, the compensation (as the law now stands) may be considerably less than the consequent loss in market value. Hence the valuer assessing site value would have to forecast not merely the most profitable new building for the site and its cost of construction but also the intentions of the local planning authority— or rather what they would be if the site were in fact going to have a new building erected on it. Such a forecast must also be made when the comparative method is used, for the 'comparable' sites will usually only have been bought when their purchasers have been promised the planning permission they need to develop their sites. This problem of the uncertainty of values under the present compensation provisions in British Town and Country Planning law would create a major difficulty in valuing sites, even though it might affect only a minority of cases, and renders the practicability of site value rating more doubtful than any other single factor. In what follows, the complication thus introduced by planning and the compensation code will, however, be disregarded. It should be noted that the same problem does not arise in the bulk of ordinary rating valuations: properties are valued in their existing state (*rebus sic stantibus*) and information on occupation rents is relatively plentiful, while equitable rules of thumb for the difficult cases have been developed over the centuries.

The Tax Change

The main features of what would seem to be the most suitable basis of assessment may now be summarized as follows:

The market value of the freehold with vacant possession free from any incumbrances other than easements and restrictions on user imposed by or under an Act of Parliament on the assumption that there are no buildings or works upon the land or anything growing except natural growth.

Under the present rating system agricultural land is not rated, industrial properties are rated at one-quarter of their annual value and dwelling-houses and flats are rated at their 1939 annual value. Thus, broadly speaking, only shops, offices and warehouses are rated on the basis of their current annual value. If site value rating were introduced in partial substitution for the present rates, it would therefore involve some degree of re-rating of various types of property. In order to avoid considering this other effect on the tax base of rating site values it will therefore be assumed (as in the previous chapter) that rates are levied on the annual value of all property at a uniform rate in the pound. The question to be examined is then what the effects would be of the introduction of a uniform national site value rate levied on occupiers accompanied by a reduction in the poundage of the present rates, such that the total revenue from rates of local authorities remains unchanged. It will be assumed that central government grants to local authorities are unchanged in total but altered in distribution so that the aggregate income and expenditure of each and every local authority is unaffected by the tax change.

Effects on Rents

The analysis of the tax change falls into two parts, the effects on rents and the effect on the amount and type of building. Firstly, the effects on rents will be considered on the assumption that there is no change in the standing stock of buildings.

Since the tax change involves no change in the total amount of rates levied on property, it will merely redistribute that amount between different properties. As both rates are assumed to be levied at a uniform rate in the pound over the whole country, the imposition of the site value rate will exactly offset the reduction in rates on annual value only in the case of those properties with a ratio of annual value to site value equal to the national average, i.e. the aggregate of annual values divided by the aggregate of site values.

The total amount of rates payable will rise in the case of those properties which have a ratio of annual value to site value below the national average. These are the properties, in other words, whose rental value on a short occupation lease stands low in relation to the price for which the freehold could be sold in the absence of any lesser interests and on the assumption that any buildings, crops, etc., on the land had disappeared into thin air.

What sorts of property are likely to fall into this category? Firstly and most obviously, properties with no or few buildings, such as vacant sites, car parks, storage grounds, playing fields, market gardens and agricultural land. The site value of these properties will not be much less than the capitalized value of their rental value for occupation. Indeed, it will be considerably more where there is an element of development value. For example, the freehold of agricultural land suitable for building on the outskirts of an expanding town will sell for an amount much in excess of the capitalized value of its agricultural rent. It is therefore absolutely certain that the tax change would involve a heavy increase in the liability to rates on such land. The same will be true of vacant urban sites, on which rates are not paid at present.

If agricultural land provided the greater part of aggregate property values, the tax change would lower the rate liability on nearly all built-on properties, including most urban properties.[1] This is presumably not the case in England, however: there would therefore be a shift of the burden of rates within urban areas as well as from urban areas to rural areas. One type of urban property which would be likely to suffer an increase in liability would be properties with obsolescent buildings due for demolition fairly soon. The reason is that it is worth while to demolish a building when the value of the site exceeds the value of the property in its present state by the cost of demolition. Thus the value of a property with a building which retains only a few years of useful life will not be much different from its site value, just like agricultural land with no building potential.

Even where, by contrast, the present building is suited to the site, the annual value of some urban properties in proportion to their site value may be below the national average for all proper-

[1] Even if agricultural land were rated, which at present it is not.

ties together. Where the level of site values is particularly high—
in the centre of large towns—the capital value of a property, and
hence also its annual value, though high in absolute terms, is
particularly low in relation to the value of a site.[1] This can be
explained in theoretical terms by taking the extreme case of
adaptation of a building to its site, namely a new building costing
the optimum outlay. In Diagram III on page 53 the annual
value of a site A is $UVWY$, while the annual value of site B is
only $URST$. The ratio of $OVWK$ (the annual value of property
A with the new building) to the former is WK/WY, which is
considerably less than the ratio for property B, SJ/ST.

The general effect of the tax change, to sum up, would therefore be a shift in the burden of rates towards unbuilt-on land,
particularly land part of the value of which represents profitable
future development potentialities, and towards urban properties
in areas of particularly high site value.

Since the tax change leaves government expenditure unchanged
and has no direct effects on investment or on personal incomes,
it will not alter the demand for accommodation. Thus the
occupiers of properties on which the rate liability is increased will
find themselves paying rent plus rates in excess of the equilibrium
amount. Thus, in the absence of rent control, as leases expire a
downward pressure on their rents will develop, and conversely
landlords will gradually push upward the rents of properties on
which rate liability has been reduced. The new equilibrium
position towards which these movements will lead will be one
where the sum of site value rate, annual value rate and rent paid
for each property equals the amount of rates on annual value
and rent in the initial equilibrium. This is an equilibrium because
incomes, tax revenues, the amount paid for accommodation
(given an unchanged standing stock of buildings) and the prices
of other goods and services will all be the same as in the initial
equilibrium.

[1] This fact is agreed upon by many of the expert witnesses who gave
evidence to the Royal Commission on Imperial and Local Taxation at the
turn of the century and to later committees of enquiry.

As will be shown below, the tax change will alter some site values, and so the poundage of the site value rate will have to be altered to maintain a constant revenue when these alterations are reflected in revaluations. There will probably need to be no such alterations in the poundage of the rate on annual value, since the aggregate of rents will not be changed even though some rents rise and others fall.

Within the period during which the effects of the tax change on building have not yet begun to be felt the main result is thus some redistribution of income from the landlords (or owner-occupiers) of property with a low ratio of annual value to site value to those whose property has a high such ratio. Any effects on the allocation of resources will be minor ones, incidental to the frictions of the process of adjustment of rents.

Effects on Building

The effects of the tax change and the changes in rents which result from it on the amount and kind of building will be examined for three types of property: vacant urban sites, agricultural and accommodation land on the fringes of an expanding town and urban properties with existing buildings.

Consider first a vacant urban site which is not used as a car park or anything like that, so that its annual value is zero and no rates are levied on it before the tax change. The Ceiling price which a potential developer will be prepared to pay for it in order to acquire it and put up a building depends upon construction costs, maintenance costs, the rent which it is anticipated could be obtained from a new building, the poundage at which rates are levied on annual value, annual value being equal (or closely related) to the rent obtainable, and the amount of rates levied on the site value. How will the tax change and its effects on rents as discussed above affect these variables?

Building costs will presumably rise or fall if building is generally encouraged or discouraged. But here it will be assumed that they are unaffected, since the effect on building has yet to be

G

ascertained. (If the supply of building effort is less than infinitely elastic, the following results still hold since a lower elasticity merely reduces the magnitude of the effects and does not alter their direction.) Maintenance costs may also be assumed to be unaffected. Thus on the side of costs there is no force acting to alter the curves of average and marginal net returns from outlay on construction on the site.

The amount which potential tenants will be prepared to pay in rent and rates together for a new building of any given type on the site will be unaffected by the tax change (save possibly during the transition period following immediately upon it). This is because the equilibrium amount of rent plus rates of existing accommodation, which would compete with the new building, is the same as before the tax change, as was shown in the last section. For the particular site, therefore, the curve ar in Diagram VII represents average returns, net of maintenance but including rates, both before and after the tax change. Subtracting rates on annual value before the tax change gives the curve A_0 as average net returns on construction outlay. If the rate of interest were OJ, the optimal outlay would be OD and the annual value of the site $JKLM$.

The reduction in the poundage of rates on annual value will raise the average net returns curve to A_1 so that the optimal outlay rises from OD to OE. Actually, since the occupier is assumed to pay the site value rate, the new average curve will lie below A_1 by the amount of the rate, but this will not affect the marginal net returns curve M_1 since the amount paid is independent of the sort of building erected. The annual site value will be $RSTJ$ minus the rate on site value. Thus if the rate on site value is levied at x per cent and annual value is capitalized in perpetuity at r per cent, the Ceiling price for the site will be

$$(RSTJ)\left(\frac{100-x}{100}\right)\frac{100}{r}.$$

This analysis produces two conclusions. Firstly, the tax change will raise the optimal outlay so that new buildings will be larger or more durable than they would have been if planned before the tax change. Secondly, the tax change may either raise or lower the value of vacant sites.

It is a little paradoxical that the introduction of a site value rate may raise site values. Perhaps an analogous case will assist

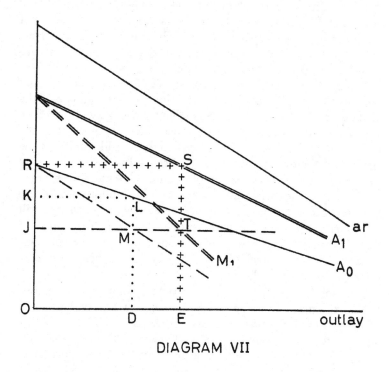

DIAGRAM VII

in understanding this. If a poll tax is substituted for an income tax in such a way that a particular person pays the same amount of tax as before, his marginal tax rate falls to zero. He will therefore earn more income so that, tax being the same as before, his disposable income rises. If the poll tax were a little bit higher, he might still end up with a disposable income larger than before the tax change.

It has been shown that if the site is developed it will be

developed more intensively than it would have been without the tax change. This leaves open the question of whether it will be developed. Suppose firstly that the potential developer owns the site. If its value is increased, this clearly represents an increase in the profitability of development and conversely if its value is decreased. But even in the latter case, so long as its value is not reduced to zero it will pay to build on the site rather than to leave it undeveloped. Thus, in either case, if development was worth while before the tax change, it will be worth while after it.

Where the owner considers selling, his Floor price will reflect the value of the site to him if he develops, or his estimate of the Ceiling prices of other developers. The tax change will therefore alter the owner's Floor price by much the same amount as the Ceiling price of a potential developer so that the likelihood of the site being sold for development is unaffected. Indeed it is increased somewhat, since the imposition of the site value rate forces a new expense upon the owner and the effect on his liquidity may cause him to expedite a sale. On balance, therefore, the tax change will have small effect on the number of vacant sites developed, if anything increasing it slightly, but the total amount of construction outlay in developing such sites will nonetheless increase, since the intensity of development will be raised.

A simpler argument will give a stronger conclusion than this. It applies equally to vacant urban sites and to land on the fringe of a town which yields some income from its existing use for agriculture, etc. The imposition of the site value rate, taken by itself, reduces the income from a property by the same amount irrespective of the use made of it. It therefore has no effect on the increment of income resulting from development. The lowering of the rates on annual values does have such an effect, however: since the annual value of the property will be greater when developed than before, when it was vacant or used for agriculture. The reduction of rates on the developed property is greater than the reduction on the undeveloped property. Thus, taken by itself, it raises the increment of income resulting from development, since lower rates mean higher rents.

The net effect of the two parts of the tax change taken together is thus to raise the profit from any given outlay on development. In addition, as argued above, the optimum outlay on development will be increased and a liquidity effect may also act to accelerate development. These three effects apply equally whether the net effect of the tax change is to raise or lower the site value of the property. These conclusions are subject to one qualification, however. Insofar as part of the outlay is directed to improving the site—e.g. by provision of access roads and sewers—the expenditure will raise the liability to site value rate. In cases where such expenditure is an important part of the whole, therefore, the tax change will discourage building and lower site values. Thus the stimulus will largely be confined to improved land unless there is some allowance for the cost of new improvements in assessing site values.

The claim of the advocates of site value rating that its partial or total substitution for the present system would result in greater development of fringe land is therefore in general correct.[1] But except insofar as liquidity difficulties cause many landowners to put their properties on the market for development, their claim that the tax change will lower the prices at which such fringe land is sold is not generally true. As has been shown, developers' ceiling prices may rise, in which case competition between them will pull up land values.

A third claim of the advocates of the rating of site values is that the tax change would check 'unsound' speculation. This is probably true, since the carrying cost of land with a high value for development will be increased. However, this will discourage all speculation, 'sound' as well as 'unsound'. The distinction between these two has not been drawn, and one may suspect that the term 'unsound' has been used pejoratively rather than descriptively. Yet it is conceivable that a person ready to hold

---

[1] Assuming that the building industry can expand. Note that when, as at present, agricultural land is not rated the effect of the tax change will be even stronger, for then the reduction of rates on annual value benefits developed properties only.

land for future development may, through his foresight, perform a useful rôle in allocating land between competing uses.

So far the analysis of the effects of the tax change upon building has excluded consideration of the redevelopment of built-up land in urban areas. It was shown in the previous section that the rents of some urban properties will rise while those of others will fall. But changes in the value of properties in their existing state do not *per se* affect the profitability of redevelopment, which depends upon the cost of redevelopment compared with the increase in the value of the property due to redevelopment. This increase, while unaffected by the site value rate, will be greater the lower is the poundage of the rates on annual value, since except when an old building is replaced by an almost identical new one, redevelopment raises the annual value of the property. The increase in rate liability due to reconstruction, enlargement or alteration of a building will generally be smaller after the tax change than before. Urban redevelopment will therefore be stimulated.

To sum up: the tax change would stimulate building, except where improvements to the site were an important part of the total cost, it would raise the site value of nearly all properties with an annual value/site value ratio above the average and it would also raise the site value of many properties with an annual value ratio below the average. These conclusions may seem paradoxical unless it is remembered that the results would be very different if the proceeds of the site value rate were used for some other purpose than to enable a reduction to be made in the poundage of the present rates.

CHAPTER VIII

FREEDOM OF CONTRACT

The Problem

THE question to be considered in this chapter is the advisability of intervention by the public authorities which either imposes some obligation not undertaken in a property contract or limits the rights of a party to a contract and which redounds to the benefit of the other party. At present in Britain intervention of this sort is well established under several different pieces of legislation. For example, under the Landlord and Tenant Act, 1927, covenants in leases which bind the lessee not to assign his lease without the lessor's permission are 'deemed to be subject to a proviso to the effect that such licence or consent is not to be unreasonably withheld'. Another example is the grant by the Landlord and Tenant Act, 1954, to the tenant of business premises of the right to a new lease when his existing term expires, so that he has security of tenure. His landlord can secure possession only on certain specified grounds, and if they cannot agree on the terms of the new tenancy the terms are decided by a court. Similar legislation, if anything more far-reaching, relates to agricultural property.

As with other problems of economic policy, the arguments for and against freedom of contract in real property transactions may be broadly classified under two heads. Firstly, there are considerations of equity and fairness as between landlord and tenant. This may be called the 'distributional' aspect of the problem, since the benefit derived from a contract by each of the parties is largely a matter of the distribution of income and wealth between them. Secondly, the other arguments relate to the 'allocational' aspect of the problem. Here, the discussion concerns not the relative gain to each of the parties, but who occupies premises and how they are used: in other words, how resources are allocated between different uses. Thus the argument that a proposed scheme is disadvantageous because it would benefit tenants sitting under recent leases less than other tenants is clearly distributional. On the other hand, the argument that granting security of tenure to shopkeepers diminishes competition in retailing is an allocational argument.

Only the allocational case for interfering with freedom of contract will be considered here; though some distributional effects are noted, they are not judged. There is the more reason for this in that most discussion of landlord and tenant law pays insufficient attention to the allocational problem. However, neglect of the distributional aspect means that the arguments of this chapter are insufficient as a foundation for policy.

A second limitation on the discussion is that residential and agricultural property is not considered, as both present great complications.[1] Thus the analysis relates only to business premises, such as shops, offices, warehouses and factories. The term 'landlord' is used to mean the owner of the interest to which the occupier's lease is subject; he may or may not be the freeholder.[2]

Professor Pigou's Argument

One argument for intervention has been stated by Professor Pigou.[3] He pointed out that the social product of an improvement

[1] Leasehold enfranchisement and the tenure of business premises were considered by the *Leasehold Committee* (Cmd. 7982, 1950). Both the majority and minority reports contain references to previous investigations. Agricultural tenure is a subject in itself and is not considered here.

[2] In the latter case he in his turn is a lessee and the lease held by the occupier is an under-lease or sub-lease. Note that the landlord may not have granted the lease to the occupier, as it may have been granted by his predecessor in title from whom he acquired his interest subject to the occupier's lease.

[3] *The Economics of Welfare*, Pt. II, Ch. IX.

to property undertaken by a tenant will exceed the private product to the tenant if the benefit from the improvement is expected to last longer than the lease under which the tenant sits. The excess of social over private product is the present value of the amount by which the landlord may expect the property to be increased in value when the lease expires in consequence of the improvement having been undertaken. The tenant will clearly lose this part of the value of his improvement if he quits when his lease expires. But he will also lose it if he obtains a new lease and stays on, for the rent will be raised against him. Evidence on this point was collected by a Select Committee of the House of Commons who formed the

'opinion that although the claims of tenants to the benefits of their improvements are frequently taken into consideration by landlords or their agents in fixing the terms of renewals of leases, yet as a rule any improvements which may have been made by the tenant are regarded as the rightful property of the landlord on the termination of the lease, and that in such cases rents are commonly raised in consequence of such improvements to the extent of either a part or the whole of the increased value they may have given to the premises'.[1]

Now, it is clearly possible for the value of the private product to be less than its cost while the value of the social product exceeds the cost. In such cases, Professor Pigou argues, the effect upon the allocation of resources is partially 'mitigated' by legislation requiring landlords to pay compensation to outgoing tenants equal in amount to any increase in the value of the property due to improvements undertaken by the tenant during his occupation. Now, this argument appears to overlook an important possibility.[2] In the cases in question, where the value of the social product exceeds the cost, the present value of the gain which will accrue to the landlord if the improvement is

[1] *Select Committee on Town Holdings* 1889. Report, p. 11.
[2] I am indebted to Sir Arnold Plant for bringing this point to my attention.

undertaken will exceed the present value of the loss the tenant incurs by undertaking it. It follows that both parties could gain by revising the existing lease in such a way that the improvement becomes profitable to the tenant. According to circumstances, they might agree to a reduction in rent for the remainder of the term; an extension of the term; a contribution to the cost by the landlord or an increase in rent, the whole cost being borne by the landlord. If the value of the social product exceeds cost (by more than necessary legal expenses), there is a gain to be shared and so the improvement will be undertaken if both parties are prepared and able to act in their own interests. Thus there is no necessity for compulsory compensation unless either landlord or tenant is unwilling or unable to agree to what would benefit him.

This argument applies equally well at the margin of expenditure since what has been said of the value of the total product and total cost can be stated in terms of increments of product and of cost. Nor is the reasoning invalidated by any divergence of expectations between landlord and tenant. For example, if the tenant hopes for a renewal of his lease when it expires, but the landlord intends to gain possession and demolish the premises, the improvement will confer no gain upon the landlord and he will not be prepared to offer any concession to encourage the tenant to undertake it. Since the impending demolition limits the useful life of the improvement to the remaining years of the lease, however, there is no social gain to be had from it over and above the gain to the tenant. Of course, uncertainty of expectations may make either party too unsure of the gain to be had from revising the lease to be prepared to offer terms sufficiently attractive to the other party. No agreement will then be reached, and the improvement will not be undertaken. But this does not mean an inefficient allocation of resources, since uncertainty—or rather the cost of reducing it—is a social cost.

Arguments similar to those regarding improvements have been put forward in relation to the goodwill created by a shopkeeper, part or all of which he would lose if he had to move. The main point put forward has been that on the renewal of leases landlords unfairly secure part of the goodwill created by tenants by demanding higher rents, but this is a distributional question. What is relevant here is whether goodwill is a social asset; if it is, an efficient allocation of resources requires that the whole gain should accrue to the shopkeeper who creates it by his efforts. Thus if it is likely that on the expiry of his lease he will lose part of his goodwill, either by having to move elsewhere or, if he stays on, by having to pay a higher rent than any other kind of tenant would offer for the premises, he will not receive the whole benefit from any goodwill he builds up. Consequently his present lease will give him little incentive to build up goodwill.

Goodwill is the difference between the value of the business as a going concern and the sum of the separate values of the various real assets which constitute it. Since any expansion of the value of the business represents an increase in gross profits relative to costs,[1] and any economy in the use of real assets means a more efficient use of resources, the creation of goodwill can be regarded in the same light as the creation of real assets.

But if this is so, surely the foregoing discussion of the creation of real assets—improvements—is applicable too. The would-be tenant who hopes or intends to build up goodwill and fears that he would lose a large part of it if he were forced to move (so that he would prefer to suffer a large increase in rent rather than move) can secure his position by taking a long lease. Unless the landlord expects shop rents to fall in the future, the tenant will have to pay more for a long-term lease than he would for a shorter term. Since the tying-up of premises to a particular use for a long period imposes a social cost by reducing the flexibility of the economic system, the fact that the rent will be higher will not interfere with the allocation of resources. Security has a cost, so it should have a price.

It may be said that a tenant desiring security of tenure may nevertheless be unable to take a long lease since he is not certain that his business will prosper. But if he wishes to leave the

---

[1] This might be the fruit of restrictive practices, but the possibilities open to a single shopkeeper are limited and may be disregarded here.

premises, he can assign the lease and sell the business to the assignee if he does not choose to carry it on elsewhere. Alternatively, he would be able to determine the lease if on taking it he had required the landlord to grant him an option to break at certain specified times during the term of the lease. It is true that a tenant will have to pay a higher rent under a lease with a one-sided option of this sort, but again, since this is the price he pays for security, it is consistent with an efficient allocation of resources.

The conclusion so far is that there is no case for intervention on allocational grounds if tenants are able to negotiate with landlords regarding all the terms of the lease instead of being faced with a take-it-or-leave-it offer.

Nonetheless, legislation requiring landlords to pay compensation to tenants, when leases expire, of an amount equal to the increase in the letting value of premises due to things done by tenants would not interfere with the allocation of resources. So long as the application of the law was well understood by both parties when negotiating a lease, any potential claim or obligation would be allowed for in settling the terms. But legislation which attempted to deal with these problems by granting tenants an automatic renewal of their leases, at the same rents, so that landlords could not obtain possession (except upon certain specified grounds) would seriously distort the allocation of resources. The reason for this is simply that rent-paying ability is superior to the *status quo* as a guide in the allocation of business premises between competing tenants. Automatic renewal would ossify the pattern of property use.

Some Other Considerations

The foregoing argument that on allocational grounds no case for intervention has been demonstrated rests upon certain assumptions. It has been supposed that landlords and tenants will accede to any proposals which are to their advantage, that they display the foresight that may be expected of intelligent men who know their business, and that subject to the convenience of custom they are prepared to modify the terms of their offers in order to reach mutually beneficial agreements. But in practice inertia, foolishness, bloody-mindedness and incompetence play their part. Also the market for accommodation is such that in times of high demand landlords can state their terms on a take-it-or-leave-it basis. In other words, rents are sufficiently inflexible for the distinction between a buyers' market and a sellers' market to be applicable, so that the bargaining power of the parties varies with the state of the market.

These features of the property market have been largely ignored in previous chapters, and properly so. On the one hand the analysis has been concerned with broad trends and general tendencies which are little affected by such matters. On the other hand the disregard of these complications made possible the simple assumptions which are necessary for theoretical analysis. But in the present context what matters is not just the basic forces operative in the bulk of cases, but the details of individual cases, for intervention has been urged to 'make the minority of bad landlords behave like good landlords'. Thus, still confining the argument to the allocation aspects of the problem, the general analysis above does not establish that no legislation is necessary to ensure that all tenants can always secure the whole of the gain arising from their efforts and expenditure.

Possible Types of Intervention

If the case for intervention is accepted, whether on allocational or distributional grounds, there are two possibilities to be considered. One is to give tenants security of tenure—with certain exceptions—at rents which exclude any element of value added by tenants, and to require landlords to pay compensation only when tenants leave. If the rents on new leases granted to tenants claiming their rights under such a scheme were fixed in a manner which resulted in rents lower than other would-be tenants were prepared to pay, this scheme would hinder rents from their function of allocating accommodation between competing users.

The alternative procedure is to require landlords to pay compensation when leases expire, whether or not the tenants wish to remain in occupation, leaving rents and occupancy to be freely determined by bargaining. Under this scheme, the compensation in respect of improvements would be the excess of the value of the premises over what it would have been had the improvements not been undertaken.[1] Such a provision was introduced in 1927 and apparently worked fairly satisfactorily. This was not the case with compensation on account of goodwill, however, for it is almost impossible to value the difference between the value of the premises and what it would have been had the tenant not accumulated goodwill.[2] An attempt to avoid the valuation difficulty by a rule of thumb basis for compensation, landlords paying some easily ascertained amount to *all* outgoing tenants, does not solve the problem, because this liability will be taken into account when rents are fixed under new leases. There is no allocational case for compensation unless it is known by tenants that they will receive an amount proportioned to the amount by which they have enhanced the value of the premises they occupy.

The discussion of the preceding pages applies equally well to the claim that landlords should be protected against tenants if some landlords are negligent or in a weak bargaining position when granting leases. There may be a case for allowing them to restrain tenants from certain actions or to claim compensation for depreciation in the value of property caused by tenants even if they have failed to reserve such rights under the leases.

Finally there is the question of whether legislation can require all landlords to permit their tenants to do such things as under-

---

[1] This would be zero, whatever the improvements, if the landlord required possession of the premises in order to demolish and rebuild them. No compensation would be payable where the tenant had agreed to undertake the improvements as a condition of the lease, for then his obligation would have been taken into account in settling the terms.

[2] See the final report of the *Leasehold Committee, op. cit.*, paras. 121-126.

take improvements, change the user of the premises or assign the lease where such permission is demonstrably not against the interest of the landlord.

Clearly it would be impossible to lay down any general specification of clauses in leases whereby the tenant covenants not to do certain things, only to do certain things or not to do certain things without permission, and to declare such clauses invalid. On the one hand this would present an insoluble problem for the draftsman. On the other hand it would enable a tenant to do things which would reduce the value of the landlord's interest. The approach must therefore be different and on the lines of some of the provisions of the Landlord and Tenant Act, 1927. A court or tribunal should be able to grant a tenant permission to undertake improvements, change the use of the premises or assign his lease without payment to the landlord (except to reimburse his legal costs), despite any provisions in the lease unless the landlord showed that he would lose, or might lose, in consequence. It might be wiser to require the tenant to prove that the landlord would not lose.

A logical step would be to go further and, for example, empower a tenant to undertake an improvement which would lower the value of the landlord's interest if he paid adequate compensation to the landlord. However, the difficulties of ascertaining the proper amount seem to rule out this possibility as a practical proposition.

CHAPTER IX

COMPENSATION AND BETTERMENT

The Problem

TOWN and country planning in the broadest sense includes a whole range of public controls over the use of property and the acquisition of property for use or development by various public authorities. Such activities as the redevelopment of slum areas, zoning, regulation of the type of building, the construction of new highways, the establishment of new towns and the control of advertisements all fall within this broad category. The present chapter is devoted to one particular problem which inevitably arises, the problem of compensation and betterment.

Where property is compulsorily acquired, for example as the site for a new school or as part of a road-widening scheme, the owners of interests in the property will be made worse off unless they are compensated. But the impact of planning upon the fortunes of property owners is not confined to the case where interests are taken from them; in addition, various measures may affect the value of interests in property without any change in ownership. Thus, if an area is zoned as a green belt and new building is prohibited, the value of sites in the area which are suitable for new housing may suffer a considerable fall. Or the requirement that new shops in a town must have a three-storey front elevation may require an outlay on construction in excess of the optimum (from the point of view of the developer) so that the value of shop sites is reduced. Such effects on property values can also be favourable, as when the provision of a new housing estate raises the value of nearby shops.

These examples demonstrate that the financial impact of town and country planning upon property owners can occur in many ways and that it can be positive as well as negative. In consequence it has to be considered whether money should be paid to those property owners made worse off and taken from those made better off. More precisely, the compensation-betterment problem consists of deciding the extent, occasion and method of paying compensation for property interests which are compulsorily acquired or depreciated in value and levying a charge on the owners of interests which are appreciated in value.

The meaning of the term 'compensation' is clear, but 'betterment' has been used in several senses. In the narrow sense, betterment means the increase in the value of neighbouring property brought about by a particular improvement, such as the construction of a new street. In the broader sense, it means 'any increase in the value of land (including the buildings thereon) arising from central or local government action, whether positive, e.g. by the execution of public works or improvements, or negative, e.g. by the imposition of restrictions on other land'.[1] In either case it is a little confusing to contrast it with 'compensation', for the complement of the latter is not the betterment itself but charges levied in respect of it while the complement of 'betterment' is 'worsement'.

Any solution to the compensation-betterment problem must specify when compensation is to be paid, who is to pay it, how it is to be financed and how it is to be assessed. Similar matters must be specified concerning any charges levied upon betterment.

Recoupment and Betterment Charges

The finance of London street improvements undertaken in the nineteenth century affords an example of a compensation-betterment scheme which is worth examining despite the lapse of time, a reasonable amount of information being available. The construction of urban motorways now would meet similar problems, and recoupment as a means of securing some share in betterment

[1] *Expert Committee on Compensation and Betterment* (the Uthwatt report), Cmd. 6386, para. 260.

H

to the public authorities can be employed in the creation of new towns as well as in various urban improvements similar to those undertaken in London.

Recoupment involves the purchase of more land than is necessary for the construction of an improvement and the subsequent resale of the surplus once the improvement is completed. The owners of property acquired for recoupment, i.e. the owners of property which is adjacent to the improvement, thus lose both their property and any betterment accruing to it as a result of the improvement, but receive compensation in the same way as those owners whose property is required for the actual construction. The fairness or unfairness of this depends upon how generously compensation is assessed. The net gain to the authority undertaking the improvement equals:

> the resale value of the property acquired for recoupment;
> + the enhancement in the resale value of remnant land[1] due to its being united with the land taken for recoupment;
> − the compensation paid for the property acquired for recoupment.

This net gain, by reducing the net cost of the improvement, will redound to the benefit of the taxpayers whose taxes finance it. Thus the distributional effect of successful recoupment is to make the owners of adjacent property worse off and taxpayers better off than they would otherwise have been.

The use of recoupment can affect the allocation of resources in three ways. Firstly, the prospect of reducing the net cost of improvements may increase the number undertaken, since local authorities in particular may be deterred from undertaking new projects on account of their cost. Secondly, the redevelopment of land adjacent to the improvement (i.e. that taken for recoupment) may be facilitated. All interests in the property taken are

---

[1] Even when no land is taken for recoupment, there may be some surplus remnants from the land taken for the improvement since the whole of a property will have to be acquired even when only a part is required for the improvement.

bought out and consequently there are no sitting tenants with leases terminating at various future dates, so that demolition and redevelopment are not postponed. More importantly, the freehold is concentrated into one hand, so that the land can be redivided into sites of an area and shape suitable for redevelopment. For example, a large number of small house sites may be amalgamated into a few sites for office blocks. Thirdly, the remnants can be amalgamated with the land taken for recoupment, thus providing it with access to the improvement. Otherwise, being small or oddly shaped, the remnants may remain vacant or be sub-optimally developed with awkward or unsightly buildings.

Before describing actual experience with recoupment in London,[1] something more should be said about the effects of the construction of a new street, or the widening of an old one, on property values in the neighbourhood. It appears that where a street improvement in London had a big effect on local property values it tended to have this effect by causing a radical change in the character of the area, so that old buildings, many of them obsolescent dwellings of a poor type, were pulled down and new ones erected, fronting on to the new or widened street and serving a different purpose. Thus a rise in ground values of the frontage land might well be associated with a fall in the existing use value of standing buildings in adjoining streets. This seems to have been the case in Soho with the construction of Charing Cross Road and Shaftesbury Avenue, completed in 1887 and 1886 respectively. Mr. Tewson, a valuer giving evidence to the House of Lords Committee on Town Improvements in 1894, said in respect of the latter:

> 'I certainly do not find that there has been any improvement in the side streets. The street itself, of course, is a great improvement, but the side streets have suffered because of that improvement. The businesses which are carried on in the side streets have lost a great deal of the custom which used to come

[1] The following account is taken from my article published in the *Review of Economic Studies*, Vol. XXI, No. 1.

from the old streets over which this now passes. . . . The new street is taken up with a different class of property. There used to be old rag shops, old clothes shops, and marine store dealers of all kinds on the line of the old street.'[1]

This fall in the value of the tenants' interests was partly due to the diversion of traffic to Shaftesbury Avenue. The vestry clerk of St. James, in pointing this out, added, 'We used to have considerable traffic up some streets which are now very little more than playgrounds; and we have found that ever since Shaftesbury Avenue has been opened these back streets have on each change of tenancy shown a reduction in rent.'[2] A further reason for the decline in rents was that the construction of the two new streets displaced a considerable number of families, which reduced the trade of local retailers, since a different class of people came instead. It was said that 'there is a great outcry in all the back neighbourhood that the customers have been driven away'.[3] The value of public houses was often reduced in this manner.

An example of betterment due to a street widening and improved access in another part of London was given in a memorandum by the Chief Valuer of the London County Council in 1903.[4] He was

'of opinion that the property on the south side of the Strand has considerably benefited by the widening of the Strand, and in support of that view witness would point out that a property now occupied by the *Daily Graphic* office, opposite St. Clement Danes Church, recently changed hands at public auction at a price which represents at least £16 per foot super for the freehold. Prior to the Council depositing their Bill,[5]

---

[1] *House of Lords Committee on Town Improvements (Betterment)*, 1894, Q. 2469-70. This Committee is referred to below as *HL*.

[2] *HL.*, Q. 3258.

[3] *HL.*, Q. 2145.

[4] *Royal Commission on London Traffic*, Vol. III, p. 317.

[5] For the Strand widening, 1898.

£10 per foot super was the highest price that had been established for property in this position. Just prior to the deposit of the Council's bill, the *Daily Graphic* property itself was sold publicly at a price which worked out between £8 and £9 per foot for the freehold.'

In some cases, however, not even the property fronting upon a widened street was benefited.

'It does not follow that because the street is wider than it has been that it is necessarily a better street for trade. I think that in London the narrow streets are very often better for trade. Take Old Bond Street for instance. I would rather, if I were a shopkeeper, be in Old Bond Street than in Regent Street, because if you are walking up or down Old Bond Street you can see . . . a shop window if it is on the other side of the way and you have only two lines of carriages to contend with. . . . The object, I think, of a retail tradesman is to get as many people as he possibly can in a street, and to keep them there as long as he can. . . . The effect of a wide street is to give facilities for quick traffic and to get the people in and out of the street as quickly as possible.'[1]

Particularly in the case of new streets, considerable redevelopment occurred in consequence of improvements, however, and this was no doubt often as much the result of a rise in the site value of properties as of a fall in their values in their existing use. In other words, alternative uses often became more profitable absolutely and not merely relatively. But this did not always happen; there were cases where an improvement led to no change of use. Thus the construction in the City of Queen Victoria Street did not affect the character of the area, as the property behind the street was not suitable for rebuilding and was already very valuable.[2] The bankers and dealers of the City could not be outbid for the famous square mile.

---

[1] *HL.*, Q. 2445 and 2448.
[2] *HL.*, Q. 1523 and 1545-7.

In the thirty-three years of its existence the Metropolitan Board of Works spent £5¼ million on street widening, £7 million on new streets and £3 million on embankments, obtaining £5¼ million recoupment. Land was first acquired for purposes of recoupment in 1876. Previously the Board had normally acquired only those properties all or part of which were required for the construction of the street. This left oddly shaped parcels of land, often very small, which made development of the front-ages difficult and unprofitable, so the Board took backland as well in order to create plots of suitable shapes and sizes fronting on to the new street. The motives for this were no doubt both the creation of usable sites and recoupment. It has been asserted that 'if it had been only a question of intercepting the benefit they would have gone very much further than they did',[1] but even so this limited recoupment added very considerably to the gross cost of property acquired.

The procedure of the Metropolitan Board of Works may now be briefly described.[2] When the necessary powers had been obtained and plans made of the property to be acquired, notices to treat were served on the owners of interests in the properties concerned. These owners then submitted claims, many of which were settled by negotiation and others by arbitration, which sometimes took quite a long time. Once the acquisition was completed the buildings were cleared and demolished (their materials sold by public auction) and contracts for the paving and other works entered into after competitive tendering. The surplus land was let on eighty-year building leases, the ground rents thus formed later being sold in many cases.

From 1872 onwards the Board was compelled by Act of Parliament to provide land for artisan dwellings when they pulled down working-class dwellings to make way for an improvement.

[1] By the deputy chairman of the L.C.C. *HL.*, Q. 1843.
[2] See *A History of London Street Improvements*, 1855-97, by P. J. Edwards, pp. 18-19.

'In making such streets as Shaftesbury Avenue and Charing Cross Road, through districts crowded with people, the obligation of seeing that, before the old houses were taken down, other accommodation for the inhabitants was provided in the neighbourhood has been so onerous, that only those who have felt the stress of the difficulty can form an adequate idea of it . . . indeed it was not until, as the result of two investigations by Select Committees of the House of Commons, the stringent conditions imposed by the original statute had been to some extent modified that the Board was eventually able to achieve what it had undertaken.'[1]

In the case of these two streets, accommodation was provided (mainly on the site of Newport market) for no less than 3,044 'persons of the labouring classes'.

Some of the biggest improvements undertaken by the Metropolitan Board were made under the Metropolitan Streets Improvement Act of 1877. For four of these projects the assistant of Andrew Young, the Chief Valuer of the London County Council, made the calculations whose results appear in the following table, which was presented in evidence to a House of Commons Select Committee on the London Improvements Bill of 1893. Andrew Young's assistant, who later became Chief Valuer of the Inland Revenue, was said to be 'acquainted with the dealings with the property, both the purchase of the property and the sale of the surplus'.[2]

These figures show that even the fairly limited recoupment engaged in by the Metropolitan Board was anything but a financial success in three cases. Andrew Young agreed that recoupment 'is most certainly not' a remunerative system, and the Chairman of the London County Council explained that 'We

[1] Report of the Metropolitan Board of Works for 1888, p. 27.
[2] Q. 1482. The minutes of evidence of this Committee, including the table presented by the L.C.C. witnesses, are available at the Records Office of the House of Lords.

have thoroughly investigated the thing and satisfied ourselves that that system in London is a failure.'[1]

	Amount Paid for Compensation, excluding Costs	Receipts from or Value of Surplus Property	Difference
	£	£	£
GRAYS INN ROAD:			
1. Actual	423,413	84,421	338,992
2. If only land required for street had been taken	285,300	32,600	252,700
3. Extra cost due to recoupment .	—	—	86,292
CHARING CROSS ROAD:			
1. Actual	690,913	180,739	510,174
2. If only land required for street had been taken	477,913	55,000	422,913
3. Extra cost due to recoupment .	—	—	87,261
SHAFTESBURY AVENUE:			
1. Actual	1,004,990	377,569	627,421
2. If only land required for street had been taken	690,990	65,000	625,990
3. Extra cost due to recoupment .	—	—	1,431
MARSHALSEA ROAD:			
1. Actual	125,928	17,413	108,515
2. If only land required for street had been taken	95,475	7,850	87,625
3. Extra cost due to recoupment .	—	—	20,890

Before an explanation of the unremunerativeness of recoupment is attempted, a few complicating factors deserve notice. The first is that the above figures exclude legal and other costs

[1] Committee on the London Improvements Bill, 1893, Q. 1481 and 412 respectively. The L.C.C. was seeking powers to levy a betterment charge, which it later obtained after the House of Lords Report of 1894 and applied in a number of cases, including Kingsway.

incurred in the purchase or sale of land, so that the loss due to recoupment is slightly understated.

A second cause of understatement is that the figures do not include the interest on the cost of land acquired for purposes of recoupment between the time of acquisition (before the improvement was commenced) and the time when this land was let on a building lease (often several years after the completion of the improvement).[1]

A third complication is that until the Metropolitan Board of Works (Money) Act, 1884, the Board were forced to sell ground rentals within ten years of their creation in order to redeem debt. Since the Board's Consolidated Stock yielded up to 1 per cent per annum less than the capitalization rate of ground rentals, and since with the passage of time the value of the reversions would become important, this meant some loss. But this factor cannot have made much difference as the sales of surplus lands from all improvements made under the Act of 1877 totalled only some £170,000 up to the end of 1884 and the Board did not choose to sell at a slower rate thereafter. Many of the ground rents were not sold; indeed, in quite a number of cases they are still in the hands of the London County Council, and as the reversions are imminent are now very valuable.

Fourthly, had property values been falling between the time of acquisition and the time when surplus lands were disposed of, the loss caused by recoupment might require no further elucidation. It does not appear, however, that purchases were concentrated in years of general prosperity or sales in years of depression. The only annual figures obtainable relate to all the street improvements made under the 1877 Act together. These are given in the accompanying table.[2] A further clue is given by the remark

---

[1] Although it is certain that the figures under the heading 'Receipts from or value of surplus property' include the value of land not sold as well as the receipts from sales, it is not clear whether or not receipts of ground rent up to 1893 are included, though this seems unlikely.

[2] Compiled from the Reports of the Metropolitan Board for the years listed.

Year	Compensation and Purchase of Property	Rents from Surplus Lands	Sale of Surplus Lands
	£	£	£
1877	200	—	—
1878	264,877	831	111
1879	615,356	10,048	6,960
1880	726,303	18,717	10,502
1881	366,629	23,189	28,733
1882	376,247	23,472	44,316
1883	412,303	26,329	40,925
1884	368,685	31,375	38,278
1885	422,333	25,781	92,334
1886	76,031	13,551	41,422
1887	87,467	13,646	32,909
1888	24,226	58,208	18,096
Total	3,740,657	—	354,586

appearing in some of the Board's Annual Reports to the effect that few plots had been let during the past year owing to the depressed state of trade, which would indicate that most plots were let in medium or good years.

Some other reason for the failure of recoupment must therefore be sought. One was suggested by Mr. Vigers, an eminent surveyor[1]:

'There is a very strange notion of carrying out these streets and it has gone from the Metropolitan Board of Works down to the County Council, that is to have a grand opening of a street. Now in my opinion that is a mistake. What you want to do is to clear part of a street if you are looking for recoupment, and make a part of it. . . . When you have done that piece begin another piece, and give the people that you are going to turn out from the next part of the street an opportunity to re-establish themselves in the neighbourhood of the

[1] *HL.*, Q. 2087.

new street; and so go on, piece by piece. If you keep the street shut up till it is finished, and you come to the end and open it, all the people that would have been your customers have been driven away and have settled in other places, and you open your shop when all the old customers are supplied. Now I say that is one main and strong reason why recoupment has not paid.'

In effect, this argument supposes that successful recoupment requires reinstatement in the new street of those people and traders who were displaced by its construction. But, as stated above, while failure to do this may well reduce existing use values in the neighbourhood, site values will only go up much if there is a change in the character of the area and such a change requires a displacement and dispersal of previous occupiers. Mr. Vigers' argument can therefore only apply to cases where the street improvement, though making an area more pleasant and easier of access, does not lead to redevelopment by way of a different class of property. In such cases, if the people displaced have settled elsewhere, the surplus land (even that fronting the new street) may not be at all easily marketable. Some further explanation is therefore required of the failure of recoupment in the cases that one would have expected to be financially successful, those where a change of use was brought about, such as Charing Cross Road and Shaftesbury Avenue.

Recoupment would have paid if the cost of the properties acquired for recoupment had been exceeded by the sum of (a) the amount received for their sites plus (b) the enhancement in the sale value of the sites that would have been surplus even if no land had been acquired for recoupment[1] due to their amalgamation with back land to form larger and better-shaped plots. (The gain in site values would then have been great enough to outweigh the loss due to the destruction of buildings on the land taken for recoupment.) This means that recoupment was less

[1] Such sites would have existed, since the Board had to acquire the whole of a property even if only part of its site was required for the street.

likely to be a financial success the less cheaply the land was acquired and the lower the price which the surplus land fetched. In order to discover more about the cases under consideration, the best way to proceed is to ask, firstly, whether the surplus land was sold at below its market value, and, secondly, whether the land acquired for purposes of recoupment was bought at above market value. Both questions can be answered affirmatively, though it is impossible to assess the extent of the divergence from market value.

The failure of the Board to secure the full market value on leasing and selling surplus land was partly due to its obligation to provide for the rehousing of working-class people who were displaced from the properties taken for recoupment.[1] The Board provided the necessary sites.

'If sites are offered for sale subject to the restriction to erect dwellings for the working class thereon, it is found that the price realized represents only a proportion of the value of the land if sold without such restriction, in addition to the depreciation of property immediately adjoining. As an example of what this loss may mean, witness desires to refer to the case of the site of Reid's brewery, situate at the junction of Gray's Inn Road and Clerkenwell Road. This site contains an area of 139,400 feet, and was purchased at its fair market value as commercial land at a cost of £200,000. Subject to the restriction as to the class of building to be erected upon it, the utmost price that could be given for it is, in witness' opinion, £44,000, so that a loss was sustained in this transaction of £156,000.'[2]

A further reason for low receipts from the sale of land was

---

[1] Those displaced from properties taken for the street works would have had to be provided for whether or not recoupment had been attempted, and the cost of rehousing them is consequently irrelevant to the profit or loss from recoupment.

[2] Andrew Young, *Royal Commission on London Traffic*, Vol. III, Appendices to Evidence, p. 316.

corruption on the part of certain officers in the Architect's department of the Board of Works. Up to February 1887,[1] surplus land was not auctioned, but let by public tender. 'A detailed valuation [was] made by the Architect of each plot, and any offers in excess [were] accepted, subject to the [Works and General Purposes] Committee being satisfied as to the responsibility of the intending tenant.'[2] But the assistants to the Architect who carried out the valuations erred on the low side and saw to it that many plots were obtained by their friends or relations, who rewarded them.

The most famous case was that of the Colonial Institute in Northumberland Avenue. In 1884 a Mr. Hobson leased the site at £560 per annum and then bought the freehold at twenty-five years' purchase, giving the Assistant Surveyor of the Board £350 as 'a piece of spontaneous generosity' (his own words). Shortly afterwards he leased the site to the Colonial Institute at £1,090 per annum and a year later sold the freehold at twenty-eight years' purchase.[3] Many other cases were alleged; for some years the Board had been referred to as the 'Metropolitan Board of Perks'! The Commissioners appointed to enquire into these allegations reported another striking example in connection with Shaftesbury Avenue, maintaining that 'It is probable that £20,000 at least might have been obtained beyond what the Board actually received' for the Pavilion site.[4]

Despite these examples, however, the general conclusion was that 'there has hitherto been no evidence that corruption or malpractice . . . affected or marred the greater part of the work which [the Board] . . . accomplished'.[5] Witnesses from the London County Council, which superseded the Board in 1889, declared

[1] Report of the Board for 1887, p. 113.

[2] Report for 1879, p. 96.

[3] *Interim Report of the Royal Commission on the Metropolitan Board of Works*, p. 18.

[4] *Interim Report*, p. 10.

[5] *Interim Report*, p. 39. The *Final Report* issued a year later (1889) merely stated that no further evidence had been forthcoming so that there was nothing to add to the *Interim Report*.

in the House of Lords Committee on Town Improvements that malfeasance was not an important cause of the failure of recoupment. It was pointed out[1] that all the plots but one in Charing Cross Road and in Marshalsea Road, and half the plots in Gray's Inn Road, were let by auction.

The second factor mentioned above, the amount that property cost on acquisition, was undoubtedly far more important than the factor just considered. Until the entry into force of the Acquisition of Land (Assessment of Compensation) Act, 1919, the Metropolitan Board and later the London County Council had to pay much more than market value. The position under the Lands Clauses Act, 1845, which was remedied by the 1919 Act embodying the recommendations of the Scott Committee, was forcefully summarized by that Committee as follows[2]:

'The absence of any definition of value in the Lands Clauses Acts and the erroneous application to particular cases of the principles of valuation originally laid down by the Courts, which have opened the door to fanciful valuations and conventional allowances; the uncertainty as to the constitution of the tribunal, the choice of which lies largely in the hands of the claimants . . . and perhaps most important of all, the provisions as to cost of proceedings, both in obtaining compulsory powers and in the assessment of compensation; —all these are elements which have contributed to the result.'

The judicial decisions referred to adopted value to the owner as the basis for compensation; in practice this was often arrived at by adding 10 per cent to a generous estimate of market value, and in the case of land with a potential development value the owner was given the benefit of the doubt. It is thus not surprising that the Committee concluded that

[1] *HL.*, p. xi. Letter from deputy chairman of the L.C.C.
[2] *Committee on the Acquisition and Valuation of Land for Public Purposes. Second Report*, 1918. Cmd. 9229, paragraph 7. The minutes of evidence were not published, and neither the Treasury, the Records Office, the Ministry of Works nor the Ministry of Local Government and Housing appear to possess the originals.

'The effect has been that promoters have found it prudent to settle claims at prices arrived at by adding to a generous estimate of the value of the property a large part of the costs which they would have to pay if the case were contested. This again has reacted upon the claims habitually put forward, and has led to a fiction of "compensation value" which has affected the verdicts of juries and even the awards of arbitrators.'

Such a 'fiction' was only to be expected when railway promoters 'very frequently give £500 more for a property than it is absolutely worth in the market, rather than go to arbitration and spend £600 or £700'.[1]

So much for the amount of compensation paid for a single interest in a property. Now, there are several interests in many properties, and under section 18 of the Lands Clauses Acts, the owners of all the interests (other than holders of tenancies from year to year, or shorter) are entitled to receive a Notice to Treat. Thus the acquisition of a single property often involved compensation to two or more owners, sometimes including, in the case of the occupying interest, compensation for trade disturbance. Compensation being very generous, it was found by the London County Council that owners sometimes even created new interests in their property when it became known that it would be required for an improvement![2] Frank Hunt explained the matter to the Royal Commission on London Traffic in answer to questions.[3] 'Directly people imagine an improvement is to be carried out in a particular district you find that a certain class of owners immediately begin to deal with their property in the way of creating fresh interests, or even selling their property at an advanced value.' For example,

'if a landlord has a property which he has let on lease with three or four or five years to run, the tenant comes to him and asks him to allow him to surrender his lease for a short term,

---

[1] *HL.*, Q. 2155.
[2] Edwards, p. 176.
[3] Vol. II, Minutes of Evidence, Q. 7259, 7262, 7271.

and to grant him a longer term at an increased rental. That is the class of dealings that we generally find, not so much that they expend money upon the property but that they create fresh interests. That is to the interest of the freeholder, and it greatly increases the trade compensation which has to be paid. . . . It is wonderful what these speculators will do.'

Claims for trade disturbance often cost the Board a good deal.

'The claimant always says that his business will be ruined if he moves or is turned out; but I have never known a case yet . . . where a tenant has suffered the slightest damage by moving from one premises to another . . . and I have been concerned in hundreds and hundreds of cases. My father was retained by the (City of London) Corporation to advise on the widening of Leadenhall Street. I think there were something like 600 business claims in that widening scheme, on every one of which we advised and actually negotiated with the claimant. Practically every one of those tenants claimed that his business would be absolutely ruined if he had to move. Every one of those tenants is still flourishing today.'[1]

The way in which compensation could add up is well illustrated in an example given in 1885 by Shaw Lefevre, then concerned with the provision of working-class housing.[2]

'I have been very desirous to take a property with a view to a public improvement, and I was told that if I took this additional house it would involve a cost of about £40,000. The rental of the house itself certainly cannot be more than £500 a year, but on making enquiries I was told that there could be no doubt that the trade compensation to the owner of this house would in one way or another mount up to £40,000. I pointed out that there were places on the other side of the street to which the owner of this property might go,

---

[1] *Select Committee of the House of Commons on Business Premises*, 1920, Q. 2844. Mr. Lang.

[2] *Royal Commission on the Housing of the Working Classes*, Q. 12641.

but I was told that the same person had been in the fortunate condition of having occupied a house on the other side of the street from which he had been dispossessed for a public improvement, and had got enormous compensation, and had landed himself in his present place; and that if his shop was now taken again for a public improvement he would probably be equally fortunate in getting another enormous compensation for having to go once more to the other side. The kind of basis upon which it was represented to me that the claim would be made was this: it was believed that his profits amounted to £3,000 or £4,000 a year; he would probably get five or six years' purchase of these profits. He would then make a claim on the ground that the compulsory removal of his premises elsewhere would necessitate a forced sale of half his stock-in-trade, and an enormous compensation would have to be paid on that account, so that in one way or another it would, including the value of the premises, mount up to £40,000.'

Given the rules as to the amount of payment for compensation, the only way to reduce the cost of acquiring land was to reduce the number of interests bought out. If the Board had been able to buy only the freehold and leasehold interests in property where the tenancy was due to expire shortly, it could have let the tenancy run out and thus avoided paying compensation for trade disturbance. This was occasionally done where property was purchased by agreement, but was not a general procedure because there was no means of ascertaining in advance the nature and term of existing leases in order to discover whether it would be cheaper.[1]

The above analysis of the reason for the financial failure of recoupment in many cases may be added to by consideration of one case, perhaps the only case, where it was a success— Northumberland Avenue. This was built under an Act of 1873; the street itself was completed in 1876 and by 1883 all the thirty-

---

[1] Edwards, pp. 172-3.

I

one plots created had been let. At twenty-five years' purchase the total value of the ground rents created was about £855,000, whereas the amount paid in compensation and purchase of property was only £685,500.[1] This difference was more than the cost of constructing the street, so that the Metropolitan Board of Works appears to have made a profit.

The main reason for this was that only forty-seven property interests were compensated, and one of these payments, £497,000 to the Duke of Northumberland for Northumberland House, accounted for a very large proportion of the total. Mr. Vigers told the House of Lords Committee that he acted as surveyor for his Lordship in connection with the sale, which was by agreement, and that 'his Lordship's desire was that too large a price was not to be put upon it. It was to be a fair market price.'[2] Thus the Metropolitan Board of Works acquired over four acres (the house, outbuildings and grounds) far more cheaply than would have been possible had they had lessees and tenants. By laying out the land for building and providing a street the Board was then able to make a developer's profit. In Shaftesbury Avenue, on the other hand, there was nothing like such estate development, the Board only took 'so much of the properties as would be absolutely required to form the street, and to give an available building frontage'.[3] Northumberland Avenue was therefore an unusual case in two ways.

The conclusions reached in the foregoing discussion may now be drawn together and summarized as follows:

(1) A street improvement is most likely to raise the value of sites along the street if it leads to a major change in the character of the neighbourhood.

---

[1] These figures are obtained from the annual reports of the Metropolitan Board of Works. The figures given by the L.C.C. comparable with those for the 1877 improvements are: compensation paid, £658,646; value of surplus land, £831,310.

[2] *HL.*, Q. 2807.

[3] From a Report dated December 14th, 1881, by the Architect to the Works and General Purposes Committee.

(2) This change may cause some depreciation in the existing use value of properties in adjoining streets.

(3) Nevertheless, even when it is confined largely to the creation of properly shaped and sized frontage plots, recoupment is unlikely to reduce the net cost of a street improvement where:

(*a*) There is a multiplicity of interests to be acquired;

(*b*) the rules of compensation are as generous to property owners as those in force up to 1919.

(4) Recoupment failed to reduce the cost of some important nineteenth-century street improvements in London.

This failure was one of the major arguments used by the London County Council when it sought powers to levy betterment charges in respect of street improvements. These powers were granted after a favourable report had been made by the House of Lords Committee on Town Improvements, and were used in the case of a number of street improvements commenced between 1895 and 1902. Little information is available about the results, but a brief description is possible.

The betterment charge was 3 per cent per annum of half the enhancement in value of the properties lying within a betterment area demarcated by the Act of Parliament which empowered the Council to undertake the improvement. The enhancement was calculated as the difference between an initial valuation and a second valuation made within a few years of the completion of the improvement. Apart from the fact that the capital value of the charge was only 50 per cent of the betterment, property owners were safeguarded by two devices, between which they could choose. On the one hand they could appeal against the amount of charge assessed on their properties and bring the matter to arbitration. On the other hand they could require the Council to purchase their properties at the initial valuation and the Council could then choose between making the purchase of abandoning its claim to a betterment charge on those properties.

In three of the improvements where a charge was levied on

betterment,[1] the total enhancement of value was assessed at £112,826. The London County Council had originally assessed it at a larger sum, but were required to purchase some properties on which the enhancement originally assessed had been approximately £25,000. In all except one of these cases they preferred to drop the charge, however. Thus the capital value of the betterment charges levied came to only £56,413, which compared very poorly with valuation costs borne by the Council of £16,997. This experience discouraged the Council, and after 1902 they no longer considered it worth while to obtain the necessary legal powers to levy a betterment charge.

Valuations, since they inevitably involve some element of hunch and guesswork, necessarily have a margin of error. The possible error in the difference between two valuations is therefore very considerable, yet there is no other way of assessing the betterment caused by an improvement. Thus to avoid overburdening the owners of bettered property, betterment cannot be charged at 100 per cent and various provisions such as those described above must be introduced by way of safeguard. The possibilities of raising money by this method are therefore severely limited.

Problems of assessing Compensation

When town and country planning involves comprehensive control of land use, as in present-day Britain, the problem of compensation acquires certain additional complexities which were not present in the case of isolated and occasional redevelopment schemes such as the London street improvements. The publication by planning authorities of development plans, a mixture of intentions, forecasts and proposals for action, provides owners with important information concerning the possibility of compulsory acquisition of their properties or the range of uses

---

[1] Tower Bridge southern approach; Tottenham Court Road at St. Giles Circus; Kingsway-Aldwych. In the latter case land was also purchased for recoupment.

for which planning permission is likely to be obtainable, and this affects property values.

Consider, firstly, the question of compulsory acquisition. Any indication that a property is likely to be acquired in the future will depress its current market value if the market considers that the compensation payable if and when it is acquired is likely to be less than its capital value to the owner. Thus, at present, the indication in a development plan of the approximate route of a proposed new street or the approximate location of a proposed new school reduces the market value of property in the neighbourhood very markedly. This fall in value affects more properties than will actually be required where the proposals are not precise so that it is uncertain just which properties will be taken. Only if the development plan exactly delimits the properties to be acquired is the fall in market values confined to no more properties than will be taken.

If, in cases such as this, it is desired to compensate the owners, two problems arise. As with the acquisition of property, there is the problem of determining the proper amount. In addition, however, there is the further problem of determining the occasion of compensation. It could be argued that no compensation should be paid until actual loss arises; i.e. until an affected interest has to be sold for some reason or another, such as to realize capital or because an occupier wishes to move. It would be difficult, however, to lay down a list of such circumstances where compensation could be claimed in advance of acquisition. An alternative device would be to enable an owner to require the planning authority either to declare that it did not require his property or to buy it at a price equal to the compensation payable on compulsory acquisition.

Alternatively, it might be considered that all the owners of interests affected deserved compensation for the depreciation in the values of their holdings. If so, to base the compensation on the depreciation due to 'the coming into force' of the plan—i.e. with reference to the date when it received legal status—would not meet the case, since values begin to fall when the proposals of the plan become known, before formal acceptance. A precise specification of the occasion of compensation would thus be difficult to make.

The problem discussed in the last three paragraphs would be obviated if compensation were assessed, and known to be assessed, on a basis which completely reimbursed an owner for all losses suffered by him on the acquisition of his property. It would also be obviated if the only parts of the plan involving compulsory acquisition made public were those which were definite in detail. But to suppress all imprecise proposals would be to suppress information which is of use to property owners contemplating the future utilization of their holdings and to prospective purchasers.

So far, the analysis has related to compensation for the actual or proposed acquisition of properties. Similar problems arise with losses to owners caused by restrictions imposed on the use of property. If, as at present, major changes of use or the erection of new buildings are not allowed without the permission of the planning authorities, the refusal of permission for a proposed development (or its grant subject to onerous conditions) may impose a considerable loss upon the owner concerned. For example, farm land which is ripe for building and for which permission to build is granted is worth far more than similar farm land on which building is prohibited.

Complete certainty of loss comes only when planning permission for development is sought and refused. But the general intentions of the planning authorities are made known in the maps and written proposals of their development plans. If an area is zoned in a plan as residential, it is clear that heavy industry will not be allowed there, so, assuming this to be the most profitable use, some loss is certain once the proposals of the plan become known (unless they are later revised). But if the planners indicate a readiness to consider allowing some light industry in the area, the full extent of the loss will not be ascertained until permission has been granted or refused for a specific proposal to build light industrial premises. Thus the problem of when compensation shall be paid arises in a particularly acute form. The value of a property may be adversely affected by the publication of a plan, by its coming into force, by indications of the manner in which the planning authorities are using their general powers to implement the intentions of the plan (such as the decisions on applications for planning permission in respect of other comparable properties), and, finally, by specific planning decisions relating to the property in question. It could be argued that any one of these four is a proper occasion for compensation.

The problem of determining the occasion of compensation is not the only one; there is also the problem of assessing the amount. To compensate at market value might seem to be a simple rule, but the uncertainties created by planning which were referred to above would make it extremely difficult in certain cases to estimate the market value of an interest which is to be compulsorily acquired. These cases arise where part of the value of the property is a 'development value'. This occurs when the value exceeds the present value of the future net income anticipated from the property in its present state and use, so that the value includes an element representing the possibility of changing the use of property or putting up a new building some time in the future, i.e. the possibility of the profitability of future development.

Under the present British system of town and country planning, major use changes and building require planning permission. Now, in the case of a farm which is zoned in a green belt it is fairly certain that permission to build houses would be unobtainable. Thus the farm can be valued by comparison with other farms which have no development value for building— even if in the absence of planning restrictions it would fetch a price well above agricultural value as building land. Again, it will be possible to estimate the value of a block of houses in a residential area which is suitable for redevelopment by building flats, if it is fairly certain that planning permission will be forthcoming. But in other cases there may be great uncertainty as to what forms of proposed development would receive planning permission. Here, planning uncertainty is added to the uncertainty which inevitably surrounds estimates of the profitability of future development. A valuation must rest upon some assumption as to what planning restrictions would be imposed in the future. Since, *ex hypothesi*, the property is being acquired now for some purpose, it will often be difficult to show that one assumption is more reasonable than any other. Evidence of the prices paid for comparable properties bought for development does not solve the valuation problem, since most buyers will have assured themselves that they can get the planning permission they require before completing their purchases. Prices actually paid thus frequently reflect a certainty that development value can be realized, whereas all that is certain regarding the property which is to be acquired is that its owner will never have a chance to develop it.

Exactly the same uncertainties will render difficult the assessment of compensation for planning restrictions (or the assessment of a charge upon betterment). So long as the amount is related to market value, it will be necessary to estimate the difference in market value before and after the occasion of compensation. Now, in many cases either the value before, or the value after, will depend upon uncertain expectations of the planning authorities' intentions, so that the estimate of the change in market value will of necessity be fairly arbitrary.

Suppose, for instance, that the occasion of compensation is the refusal of permission for development. The market value the property had before refusal will partly depend upon how highly the likelihood of planning permission being granted was estimated. If, on the other hand, the occasion of compensation is the publication of a development plan, the value after will be less or more certain the less or more specific are the proposals of the development plan. Only if development plans specify in complete detail what will be allowed in respect of each property will the estimate of the change in value be subject to no more uncertainty than inevitably attaches to any assessment of the future.

The requirement that planning authorities should specify their intentions in respect of each and every property is clearly impracticable. Firstly, it would impart an undue rigidity to plans. Secondly, it would involve an enormous amount of work to decide and lay down exactly what would and what would not be allowed. Much of this work would be wasted, since during the currency of any plan, planning permission would be sought in respect of only a fraction of the properties covered.

These difficulties in the way of assessing compensation upon a market value basis have been regarded as constituting an argument in favour of some other approach. In addition it has been maintained that compensation equal to market value would in some sense be too generous in the case of properties with a development value. An official committee reported in 1918 that[1] 'merely hypothetical and often highly speculative elements of value which had no real existence . . . crept into awards as if they were actual; while elements of remote future value . . . too often [were] inadequately discounted and valued as if they were a readily available market'. Now, this may seem to involve merely the question of the onus of proof: it is obviously difficult for an acquiring authority to demonstrate that a claim put in by the owner of a property to be acquired overestimates the profitability and likelihood of future development. But the Uthwatt Committee on Compensation and Betterment evidently considered that there was a more fundamental reason for over-valuation, as the following passage suggests[2]:

'Potential development value is by nature speculative. The hoped-for building may take place on the particular piece of land in question, or it may take place elsewhere; it may come within five years, or it may be twenty-five years or more before the turn of the particular piece of land to be built upon arrives. The present value at any time of the potential value of a piece of land is obtained by estimating whether and when develop-

[1] *Scott Committee on the Acquisition and Valuation of Land for Public Purposes* (Cmd. 9229), para. 8.
[2] Cmd. 6386, 1942, paras. 23-4.

ment is likely to take place, including an estimate of the risk that other competing land may secure prior turn. If we assume a town gradually spreading outwards, where the fringe land on the north, south, east and west is all equally available for development, each of the owners of such fringe land to the north, south, east and west will claim equally that the next development will "settle" on his land. Yet the average annual rate of development demand of past years may show that the quantum of demand is only enough to absorb the area of one side within such a period of the future as commands a present value.

'Potential value is necessarily a "floating value" and it is impossible to predict with certainty where the "float" will settle as sites are actually required for purposes of development. When a piece of undeveloped land is compulsorily acquired, or development upon it is prohibited, the owner receives compensation for the loss of the value of a probability of the floating demand settling upon his piece of land. The probability is not capable of arithmetical quantification. In practice where this process is repeated indefinitely over a large area the sum of the probabilities as estimated greatly exceeds the actual possibilities because the "float" limited as it is to actually occurring demands, can only settle on a proportion of the whole area. There is therefore overvaluation. To quote from the evidence submitted to us by one of the professional bodies:

"One of the reasons for this over-valuation is that when any single piece of land is being considered, the prospect that building development may come its way and none other must be taken into account. This 'floating value', as it has been called, may attach to many pieces of undeveloped land on the outskirts of a town when they are considered as separate units. When considered together or 'globally' each and every unit cannot in fact secure this 'floating value' to itself, because that would assume that the demand for building land would settle upon all the units simultaneously.

Such demand, however, is in fact neither 'global' nor simultaneous; it settles upon different pieces of land at different dates. Hence the 'global' method of valuation cannot assume, at the date on which the valuation is made, the possibility that demand will settle upon all the units at that date. Therefore the 'global' valuation must be less than the aggregate of the individual valuations when considered separately."

'To quote further from the same source:

"It is obvious that no purchaser of the whole of the development rights in any complete region would pay more than the intrinsic value of such rights; and such value would be exceeded if the total possible demand were artificially increased so as to include the possibility that the 'floating value' might settle at more points, or to a greater degree, than in fact it can."'

Despite its authoritative tone, this argument is not entirely convincing. If it means more than that claims for compensation were put at too high a level by the claimants it could be taken to imply that the prices at which building land actually changed hands normally represented an over-estimate of the imminence and likelihood of development. But it is very difficult to believe that this can ever generally have been the case except possibly at the height of a building boom. No doubt some purchasers made good bargains and some made poor bargains, yet if the latter had predominated, purchasers of land with a prospective building value must have made heavy losses in the aggregate, and it does not appear to have been suggested that such was the case.

If it be agreed that the average purchaser was not over-optimistic, another explanation must be sought by asking whether the prices paid for building land might have been lower had more such land been offered for sale. Indeed this seems plausible. During any one year only a fraction of the land suitable for building in the outskirts of a town is actually put on the market by its owners. The supply of building land in one sense is thus limited, so the probability of its being built upon soon is fairly high and its price will reflect this fact. Thus to use this price to estimate the value of other comparable sites is permissible if only a few of these other sites are assumed to be up for sale, but would overstate the amount they would fetch if many were put on the market simultaneously.

It will be noted that this explanation implies that landowners hold land off the market in the sense that they are not prepared to sell or lease agricultural land for building as soon as it can be sold at a price in excess of its agricultural value. Now, while the allegation that building land was often held off the market has frequently been made by the advocates of site value rating, it has been repeatedly denied by various eminent surveyors before official committees. The above explanation of floating value is therefore only a tentative hypothesis in the absence of sufficient information on the matter. But whether or not it is correct, the idea of floating value played a big part in the deliberations which led to the initiation of a radically new compensation-betterment scheme.

Compensation and Betterment under the 1947 Act

Comprehensive town and country planning was introduced after the war in Britain, and the 1947 Town and Country Planning Act established an ingenious compensation-betterment scheme with the device of development charges.[1] The basic principle of the financial provisions of the 1947 Act was very simple: nationalization of the development value[2] of land so that private owners were to keep only the value of their real property in its existing use. Private transactions in land were consequently supposed to take place at existing-use value. The following main

---

[1] The following account is taken from my article published in *The Economic Journal*, June 1953.

[2] The development value of a piece of land is the amount it is expected to be worth if and when it is developed less the cost of development, appropriately discounted for the futurity and uncertainty of the development, minus the present existing-use value of the land.

financial provisions of the Act were obviously consistent with this basic principle:

(*a*) The price paid for land on compulsory purchase (by local authorities, statutory undertakers, etc.) was limited to its value in its existing use.

(*b*) No compensation was to be payable on the imposition of planning restrictions except when they diminished the value of land below its value in its existing use.

(*c*) When land use was changed, or land built on, a development charge could be levied equal to the consequential increase in the value of the property.

Furthermore, £300 million in Government stock (plus accrued interest in cash) was to be paid as compensation by July 1, 1953, to landowners who filed claims for loss of development rights in their property.

Development charges were paid not only by private developers but also by local authorities in respect of development on land acquired since July 1, 1948, which was the 'appointed day' when the bulk of the Act came into force. But if we lump together the central government and the local authorities, these payments cancel out; the net financial result to them together as compared to the pre-war system was composed of the following main items:

They now paid hardly any compensation for planning restrictions;

They purchased land at its existing use value instead of at its free market value including development value;

They received development charges;

They were to pay interest to landowners on £300 million.

A justification of the nationalization of the development value of land as being an improvement upon the financial provisions of the 1932 Town and Country Planning Act must therefore have rested on the following propositions:

(1) For any given amount of planning activity the net financial result just mentioned was favourable to local authorities and the government together (i.e. it was unfavourable to property owners) and ought to have been so; and/or

(2) Insofar as the amount of planning activity is influenced by financial considerations the new system was more likely to encourage the 'right' amount of planning activity than the 1932 Act:

provided that

(3) The incidental effects of the system were not so undesirable as to offset these advantages.

In order to examine the effects of Development Charges, the system must now be briefly described. Development, upon which Development Charges were levied, is defined in the Act as 'the carrying out of building, engineering, mining or other operations in, on, over or under land, or the making of any material change in the use of any buildings or other land'. Not all development was charged, however; apart from transitional provisions (and the provisions relating to statutory undertakers, local authorities, charities, etc.), the following main kinds of private development were free of charge:

Operations
  Erection of plant and machinery within a building.
  Repairs and maintenance.
  Building and erecting for agriculture or forestry.
  Erection of advertisements, fences, walls and gates.
  Rebuilding, enlarging or improving a building if this did not increase its cubic content by more than 10 per cent (or, in the case of dwelling-houses, by 7,500 cubic feet if this were greater) of its cubic content on July 1, 1948, or (if later) when first built.
  Erection, alteration or extension of buildings on property certified by the Minister as dead ripe for the development in question.

Change of Use

Increase in one use in a multi-use property by not more than 10 per cent.

Display of advertisements, camping, temporary use.

Change of use to agriculture or forestry.

Change of use within certain specified 'use classes', and certain changes from one use class to another.

Examples of chargeable changes of use were: light industrial building to general industrial building; shop to wholesale warehouse; house to hotel; boarding school to social centre. Examples of changes of use which were free of charge were: shop to office; bone burning to blood boiling; nursing home to hospital; one general industrial use to another general industrial use or to a light industrial use.

This gives a broad idea of what was liable to charge (though it was possible for development which was liable to be assessed with a nil charge on valuation grounds). The principle of assessment must now be described. This was laid down by a Statutory Regulation which required that:

'Development charge shall not be more than the . . . additional value, measured by normal processes of valuation, of the land due to planning permission for a particular development' and not less than this unless it 'ought properly to be less in order to comply with the Governing Principle' that 'land can be freely bought and sold . . . in the open market at a price neither greater nor less than its value for its existing use.'

The Central Land Board, which, working with the valuers of the Inland Revenue, was responsible for assessing and collecting development charges, reformulated the first part of this by saying that development charge was to equal the difference between the consent value and the refusal value of the land, where:

Consent Value was the value of the land on the assumption that its owner might carry out any development which was not liable to charge and the particular development for which he had planning permission, i.e. it excluded all other development for which planning permission was required.

Refusal Value was the value of the land on the assumption that its owner might carry out any development which was not liable to charge but that all other operations and uses were permanently prohibited. For present purposes this can also be called existing-use value.[1]

Development charge was thus to be 100 per cent of the increase in capital value due to planning permission to develop. There were, however, a number of reasons why development charges were assessed at a lower level than that which would remove all incentive to develop.

(1) Value was taken as being the price land would fetch if offered for sale in the open market and not as including 'the whole of the profit-earning capacity of the land in the hands of the owner'.[2] Where there is competition in the sense that a number of properties suitable for a particular type of development are available, it is often possible to buy any one of them at a price considerably less than its full profit-earning capacity for development.

(2) Regard was had to developer's risk and profit. In the arithmetic which constituted or explained the assessment of consent value this was done in a number of alternative ways. Thus, if similar adjacent land free of charge had sold at £x per acre and this figure was taken as the consent value, the charge allowed the developer roughly the same profit as the developers of this adjacent land expected to receive when they paid £x per acre. Alternatively, consent value might be estimated by subtracting the cost of development plus an allowance for risk and profit from the present value of the developed property. Or the rate of interest at which the expected returns were capitalized to

---

[1] In some cases existing-use value as refusal value differed from existing-use value as the price paid on compulsory acquisition, but such differences are not important in the present context.

[2] *Practice Notes*, p. 11. These notes were published by H.M.S.O. for the Central Land Board.

obtain the present value might allow an adequate rate of return to the developer.

(3) 'It is realized that values may at the present time be considerably affected by the possession or otherwise of a building licence. Consent values will not be assessed at the higher figure which might result if the land were being sold with a licence attached to it in a market of potential developers who had no building licences, but could obtain one by buying the particular land with its planning permission. On the other hand, they will not be assessed at the depressed figure which might result if the land were being sold in a market composed solely of bidders unlikely to get a licence.'[1] This means that when building licences existed and had a 'scarcity value' development charges could not make development unprofitable.

(4) The 10 per cent 'tolerance' which was free of charge on rebuilding, improving, enlarging or changing the proportions of various uses in a building in many cases raised the refusal value above the existing-use value in its narrow sense, so that other factors apart, the charge tended to be less than the development value.

Development charges were an arbitrary fee in that there was legitimate room for disagreement as to the figures to be placed on the refusal and consent values of a property. Even in a pre-Act valuation of a property, say for sale, a divergence of up to 15 per cent between the estimates of two valuers was no reflection on their competence. But in the absence of useful information about rents paid, the estimation of a refusal value was extremely difficult, since land very rarely changes hands at existing-use value (refusal value) where it has any development potential. Nor was consent value much easier to estimate; it is revealing that the rents paid for factory space in the New Towns were sometimes used in the South of England as a basis for assessing the consent value for factories of land elsewhere. And where a consent value was reached by deducting the cost of development from the present value of the expected rental value of the developed

[1] *Ibid.*, p. 19.

K

property, a small change in the expected future rental value per foot of floor space might make a big difference in the development charge. Furthermore, there was room for considerable ingenuity in securing that the part of a proposed extension which was allowed as being within the 10 per cent tolerance[1] was the most valuable part.

It is evident that there was considerable room for argument between a developer and a district valuer. The Central Land Board said:[2] 'The process is not so much one of bargaining, as has been suggested, but rather of investigating merits in the light of all available information.' Many developers, however, regarded this process as one where they used every argument they could think of to induce the district valuer to lower his figure. But the approach of different district valuers could differ, and there were cases where a developer and district valuer spent several hours trying to get the charge as low as possible. Also, it was argued that just because there was no appeal against a determination of development charge, district valuers were more generous than they would have been had a right of appeal been instituted. Lastly, when a district valuer was asked to give an informal preliminary indication, prior to formal determination, of development charge, he would obviously prefer to err by giving too high a figure rather than too low a figure, since it was much easier to reduce it later on than to raise it.

Development charge had normally to be paid in a single capital sum before development commenced, although in order that protracted negotiations should not hold up development the Central Land Board occasionally accepted a covenant to pay the charge as finally determined. The disadvantageous effect of this upon the developer's liquidity was removed in many cases from May 1952 when developers were allowed to set off charge to an amount not exceeding 80 per cent of their agreed claim upon the £300 million compensation fund against that claim. In the case of certain single-house plots and 'near-ripe' land owned by

[1] I.e. exempt from charge.
[2] Second Annual Report, p. 6.

builders which had been promised 100 per cent compensation for loss of development rights, a complete offset was allowed. But if the Treasury scheme for the distribution of the £300 million (in Government stock) had been introduced in July 1953, as was provided, offsetting would have no longer been possible.

In cases where the developer had to acquire the land which he developed there are some additional factors to be considered. It was one of the principles of the Act that the development value of land was taken out of private ownership (£300 million being granted as compensation) so that it had to be bought back by developers from the Central Land Board, the fee being the development charge. As a corollary of this the 'Governing Principle' of the Development Charge Regulations was that 'so far as is practicable' land should freely change hands at existing-use value.[1] Since this was normally the same as refusal value, the aim was that the total amount paid in purchase price and development charge by a developer should be the consent value of the land, which was rarely more than the price he would have paid in the absence of the Act. In fact, however, private sales of land with any development potential at existing-use value were the exception, not the rule. This requires discussion, firstly, of why owners often would not (and will not) willingly dispose of land at existing-use value, and, secondly, of why developers were prepared to pay more than existing-use value despite the charge.

The case of the vendor (or grantor of a long lease) is simple.[2] For an investor-owner Floor price approximates to existing-use value, if he capitalizes the returns from the property at the market rate for the type of property in question, provided that

---

[1] Except where (a) the vendor accepted liability for development charge; (b) near-ripe and single-plot land was sold; (c) where local authorities and statutory undertakers disposed of land they had previously been using, in which case the 'prevailing use' was free of charge; and (d) dead-ripe land was sold.

[2] The complications of assignment of the compensation claim and uncertainty regarding the future of the Act are mentioned later on.

the present value of the reversion includes no potential development value. In the case of owner-occupiers, a possible reason for
unwillingness to sell at existing-use value is that they may suffer
severance, disturbance, injurious affection or temporary loss of
profits, depending on circumstances. The Central Land Board,
however, stated that it would 'in such cases make a proper
allowance in arriving at the development charge'.[1] If this
allowance included such a sum as was necessary to compensate
the owner for the bother and inconvenience caused by surrender-
ing his property as well as for all the pecuniary loss involved, no
difficulty need have arisen under this head.

Where a property had some development value, however, the
owner would, when development charge existed, only have been
prepared to sell at existing-use value (i.e. at a price reflecting no
part of the development value) if he expected that the charge he
would have to pay if he undertook development himself would
completely deprive him of all development value. In other words,
if development charges were high enough for owners of properties with a development value to be willing to sell those properties
at existing-use value, they would have had to be high enough to
make the development of those properties by their owners unprofitable. This, however, does not necessarily mean that charges
at such a level would make development unprofitable to the
specialist developer, since the latter will frequently possess
greater knowledge and skill than the ordinary landowner.

The Central Land Board listed three reasons why developers
should have been unwilling to purchase land at more than its
existing-use value[2]:

'(1) No compensation is generally payable on refusal of
planning permission. Thus, if a person buys land above
existing-use value and fails to get planning permission for
further development, he will be out of pocket on the deal.

'(2) The development charge will not be assessed at a lower
figure because a purchase has taken place above existing-use

[1] *Practice Notes*, p. 19.   [2] *Ibid.*, p. 2.

value. Thus, again, such a purchaser will pay more than he should.

'(3) Most compulsory purchases, including those of the Central Land Board, are to be at existing-use value. So yet again a previous purchaser at a higher figure will be a loser.'

The first reason cannot have been very important: a developer who knows his business will not acquire land unless he is fairly certain that he can get planning permission. Nor could the fear of compulsory purchase have been very significant; it is possible to discover whether acquisition by a local authority, if not by a statutory undertaker, is likely, while the compulsory purchase powers of the Central Land Board were rarely exercised, and then only where an owner would not sell at existing-use value to a developer.

This leaves the second reason, and here the point is not how much the developer 'should' have paid but how much he could afford to pay. If the maximum amount he would have paid for the developed property rather than go without it minus the cost and normal profit of the development operations was $£a$, and the consent value was $£b$, then he would have preferred to pay up to $£a - £b$ above refusal value for the land than not develop. But such an excess normally existed, as shown above.[1] If this excess were less than the minimum excess above existing-use value at which the present owner of the land would sell it, then the charge would have prevented development. If it were greater, then the charge would not have abolished, but only reduced, the

---

[1] The following extract is from p. 10 of the second report of the Central Land Board: 'Building licences are difficult to get and the developer who has been fortunate enough to obtain one is often willing to pay a much inflated price for a piece of land upon which to build. In other words a "scarcity value" attaches at present to the possession of a licence. The theory that the development charge would leave the developer unwilling or unable to pay more than existing-use value for his land is not at present working out in practice, especially since a would-be house-owner who pays building value to the seller of the land, as well as a development charge to the Board, is still paying less in the total cost of his house than he would have to pay for an existing house with vacant possession.'

profitability of the development. Even so, however, the existence of the charge might have caused the developer to go elsewhere if there were an alternative property available the existing use of which was the same as the developer's proposed use so that the charge on it would be nil (unless there were an extension above the 10 per cent tolerance). Thus, whereas without the Act a developer wishing to build a factory might prefer site 1 (heath) to site 2 (bombed factory), development charges might have led him to locate on site 2.

Another factor must now be mentioned. While many owners sold at prices much in excess of existing-use value,[1] others held their land off the market altogether for two reasons. Firstly, the Central Land Board only exercised its power of compulsory purchase where the owner of land had actually offered to sell (at a price above existing-use value). Secondly, in the early days of the Act people were waiting to see how it would work; later they waited to see how it would be altered.[2] Lastly, there is a reason in a different category from those so far discussed why more than existing-use value was paid for land. This is that the vendor (or lessor) sometimes assigned his claim on the £300 million. In the early days of the Act the general expectation was that such claims were worth very little[3]; the transfer of them served as an excuse for the high price. When expectations became more definite and more optimistic, they probably figured more explicitly in negotiations and in the price paid. Later still, the expectation that the

---

[1] It may be noted that since land capable of development changed hands at prices above refusal value and below consent value, the records of many current transactions were of no help to district valuers in assessing development charges. Since sales free of charge of single plots and builders' near-ripe land were to cease in January 1953 and since pre-Act values were becoming more and more out of date, it follows that the assessment of charges would have become more arbitrary.

[2] When it appeared that the average rate of payment on compensation claims would be 80 per cent, owners became less likely to sell for liquidity reasons.

[3] In January 1951 a claim for £4,193 was sold by auction for £220; other sales took place at 2s. 6d. in the pound.

financial provisions would be altered again caused uncertainty as to the worth of claims.

What were the effects of the system upon the amount and kind of development? It seems very likely that it affected the type of development, increasing the proportion which was not liable to charge, that is chiefly agricultural improvements, the rebuilding of buildings without any change in use, small extensions of existing buildings and the conversion of big houses into flats. Secondly, the complexity and uncertainty of the system together with the expectation that it would be altered, probably checked, or at least deferred some development, both by owners and, more particularly, when the developer had to acquire the land. In this latter case, as explained above, many landowners refused to sell: rather than ask a price well in excess of existing use value, they kept their land off the market altogether.

Of these two effects the former was presumably the more important, since with the building industry fully extended the total volume of construction work could not have been much greater. Thus any check on development must have been primarily a matter of changes of use. Had the system been continued, however, restrictive effects of development charges might have become apparent, but the charges were abolished.

The 1954 Act

From January 1955 the rules of compensation have been fixed by the Town and Country Planning Act, 1954. This Act makes use of the claims for loss of development value which were established under the Act of 1947 and were to have served for apportioning the £300 million of compensation. To explain this,[1]

---

[1] The following account is taken from my article published in the *London and Cambridge Economic Bulletin, Times Review of Industry,* September 1955. The exposition ignores all problems of apportioning value which arise from (*a*) multiplicity of interests in a property; (*b*) splitting or combination of properties since 1948; and (*c*) acquisition or planning restriction relating to only a part of a property.

it is necessary to define the term *Original unexpended balance of established development value.* This is the amount determined under the 1947 Act (if above a minimum amount) as the development value in 1947 of a property *less* any amounts paid in respect of that property under the retrospective provisions of the 1954 Act *plus* one-seventh of the remainder (equivalent to interest net of tax from 1947 to 1954).

The retrospective provisions of the 1954 Act are designed to 'unscramble' the superseded financial provisions of the 1947 Act. Payment will be made to owners of land with an established 1947 development value who paid development charge, sold their land at existing-use value or were refused permission to undertake new development. These payments thus reimburse owners who had the 1947 development value of their property taken from them in one way or another; very broadly, the effect will be to make things as they would have been if the present system had been part of the 1947 Act.[1]

The unexpended balance at any time is the amount of the Original unexpended balance of established development value left over and available for compensation. It is thus the Original balance less (*a*) any amounts paid in compensation from it and (*b*) the development value of any development undertaken since 1948. Thus the balance will be reduced and finally extinguished by compensation when new development is not allowed and/or by the value of new development when it is allowed. It will be extinguished if the land is compulsorily acquired.

Where there is no unexpended balance, compensation is (in principle) fairly simple. If the land is acquired, compensation is limited to the existing-use value (plus an amount for disturbance where an occupying interest is acquired).[2] No compensation at

---

[1] Development charge paid on land without a 1947 development value will not be refunded. Thus the developer of such land *is* worse off than he would have been had the system of development charges never existed.

[2] And, in some cases, severance and injurious affection. These are only important where *part* of a property is acquired, so are neglected here, in accordance with footnote 1, p. 141.

all is paid for planning restrictions unless they interfere with existing use. Thus, if permission is refused to undertake new development of a property, the owner receives no compensation at all, however big its present development value, if there is no unexpended balance attached to it.

Where there is an unexpended balance, compensation for compulsory acquisition equals the existing-use value plus the unexpended balance. In addition, where works on the land have been begun but not completed, so that the new 'existing-use' is not yet achieved, extra payment will be made equal to the value of these works.

Where planning permission for new development is refused (or granted subject to conditions which reduce its profitability) for land with an unexpended balance, compensation is to be whichever is the lesser of the unexpended balance or the depreciation in the value of the property. However, even where the planning decision does impose a loss, compensation is excluded in a whole range of cases, however large the unexpended balance. The following are the most important exclusions:

(a) Refusal of planning permission for a change of use, which involves no major building operations.

(b) Refusal of permission to display advertisements.

(c) Imposition of conditions relating to layout, size, construction and appearance of buildings when planning permission is granted.

(d) Refusal of planning permission for new development on the grounds that the development would be premature in terms of the development plan or deficiency in the provision of water supply or sewerage.

(e) Refusal of permission for new development if the applicant is promised permission instead for alternative development of a residential commercial, or industrial character.

This list of exclusions is formidable. It would seem not only to cover the imposition of restrictions on grounds of good neighbourliness but also to allow planning authorities to avoid compensation in other cases by granting permission for some alternative but not equally remunerative development. For example, if an authority felt really nasty and the Minister backed it up, it could prevent erection of an office block without compensation by granting permission only on conditions which would render it unprofitable—e.g. a very low density and extensive car-parking requirements. All restrictions have to be reviewed by the Ministry, however, as compensation for planning restrictions on new development is to be paid by the Ministry, not by the local planning authority. Furthermore, the authority's intentions must be assumed to be reasonable, and informal discussions between the developer and the planning officer usually precede the formal decision. The reasons why the possible exclusions are nevertheless so extensive are partly to avoid payment where an owner applies for planning permission in the hope of refusal merely to get compensation, and partly the same as the reason for the remarkable complexity of other parts of the Act: the draftsmen wished to cover every possible contingency. Their aim was to specify what could happen, not what would happen. Those who criticize the Act should endeavour to redraft it more simply and see whether they can avoid possible anomalies without creating inevitable ones. It is, of course, true that a great deal of discretion is given to the authorities, but this is no unique feature of planning law.

It follows that until experience of the working of the Act is accumulated it should be judged on its intentions rather than on its possibilities. In the part under consideration—compensation for restrictions on new development on property with an unexpended balance—the intention seems to be to pay little or no compensation except when an owner is both prevented from new development which is not deemed to be directly anti-social and also not allowed to use his property for any alternative reasonably remunerative urban use. Compensation will clearly be paid if building on green land which is ripe for development is prohibited. It will not be paid, for example, if a house is not allowed to be used for offices, if flats are required to contain an underground garage, or if a factory is prohibited in a residential area.

A major complaint against the Act on grounds of fairness has been that it discriminates between property owners. Where new development is permitted or where urban changes cause existing-use value to rise, the owner gets the gain. On the other hand, where land is compulsorily acquired, the owner suffers a loss if its current development value exceeds the unexpended balance (if any); and, where permission for new development is refused, he suffers a loss if the depreciation in the value of his property exceeds the compensation (if any).

In defence, two points have been made. Firstly, some at least of the exclusions from compensation where there is an unexpended balance relate to restrictions imposed in the interest of the community which are a matter of 'good neighbourliness', and these do not deserve compensation. Secondly, it has been urged that the fairness of the compensation provisions should not be judged *in abstracto* but by reference to the expectations established under the 1947 Act. According to this approach, therefore, owners only have cause to complain if they are worse off than they would have been had development charges not been repealed and the 1954 Act not been passed. Now, the major differences are as follows:

(*a*) Where permission is granted for new development no development charge is paid, so the owner is better off unless the charge would have been less than his share in the £300 million payment for loss of 1947-development value. (This £300 million was to have been distributed among owners in 1953 according to the 1947 development of their properties; most owners would have received an amount equal to 80 per cent of their agreed claim for loss of development value.)

(*b*) Where land is acquired, although the compensation is roughly the same, compensation above existing-use value is the whole of the unexpended balance, paid on acquisition, instead of some 80 per cent of it which would have been paid in 1953.

(c) Similarly where planning permission is refused, except for the exclusions under the 1954 Act.

(d) Other owners (whose land is not acquired and who do not apply for permission for new development) get no payment for loss of development value, whereas under the old Act they would have received some in 1953.

Those deprived of compensation under the exclusions of the new Act would have received their share of the £300 million in 1953. Otherwise only the fourth class of owners are substantially worse off under the new system, and it has been said that they did not deserve payment for loss of what they were not going to realize.

Whatever the merits of the above argument, it has not convinced all commentators on the new Act, and many of them think it wrong that an owner may have his land acquired at a price which, when the property has a substantial development value at the time of acquisition, may be much less than market value.

This possibility and the limitations on compensation for refusal of planning permission for new development will clearly make developers unwilling to purchase land for new development unless they are assured of planning permission and of freedom from compulsory acquisition. The Act provides a safeguard in respect of the latter by requiring local authorities to pay full market value if they acquire land within five years of a prospective purchaser asking for and receiving an assurance that there is no intention to acquire that land compulsorily within five years. Thus a would-be purchaser will not conclude a purchase until he has both this assurance and planning permission (and an Industrial Development Certificate from the Board of Trade where necessary). Purchase of land much in advance in development will be risky, however, and probably rare. It will often be in the interest of an owner wishing to sell or lease land capable of development to obtain an outline planning permission before offering his land for sale.

Where compulsory purchase is likely, rather than merely a possibility, land may become very difficult to sell, even if it has no development value. Even though in such cases compensation is at full market value and in addition compensation is payable for disturbance to the occupier, acquisition is apparently regarded as causing a loss. Development plans designate certain sites for compulsory acquisition within ten years, and Ministerial approval of plans is a preliminary authority for these acquisitions. The Act provides, however, that depreciation of value due to such designation is to be disregarded in assessing compensation, i.e. the property is to be valued as though it had not been designated. Difficulties arise with less definite proposals in a plan. These include the indication of a proposed school or open space or clinic by a symbol on the development plan. Such a symbol merely means that, for example, a school is thought to be needed thereabouts. Similarly, the route of a proposed new road is roughly indicated by a wide band. The market takes the view that if a property is under such a symbol or line on the map this means that the property may be acquired some time. Consequently the property becomes saleable only at a very low value, which inflicts hardship on an owner who needs to sell.

One partial remedy for this is now being followed, to restrict indication of intentions to those which are fairly definite and not too remote. A second remedy is for the planning authority to purchase the property in advance where difficulty arises, but at present no general sanction for such purposes is made by the Ministry.

The two major complaints against the new system which have been noted are its complexity with the resulting uncertainty about its working, which is more than just a nuisance, and compensation for compulsory acquisition on a basis other than market value. As regards the first point, only the accumulation of experience will show whether these difficulties are inherent in the system or merely transitory. As regards the second point, the argument is a distributional one. The proposed alternative, compensation at market value, is not without its difficulties however, as was shown earlier in this chapter. Although much can be learned from past experience it therefore seems that the compensation-betterment problem has yet to be solved satisfactorily.

INDEX

THE END

Printed in the United States
by Baker & Taylor Publisher Services